The Inmos Saga

THE INMOS SAGA

Mick McLean and Tom Rowland

Q

Quorum Books
Westport, Connecticut   London, England

Library of Congress Cataloging in Publication Data

McLean, Mick.
   The Inmos saga.

   1. Electronic industries — Government policy —
Great Britain.   I. Rowland, Tom.   II. Title.
HD9696.A3G676   1985   338.4′76213817′0941   85–24441
ISBN   0–89930–165–7

First published 1985

Published in the United States and Canada by
Quorum Books, a division of Greenwood Press,
Westport, Connecticut

English language edition, except the United States and Canada,
published by Frances Pinter (Publishers) Limited

Library of Congress Catalog Card Number: 85–24441

ISBN: 0–89930–165–7

Printed in Great Britain

Contents

Foreword

It is impossible to appreciate the full subtlety of the saga of Inmos without understanding at least a little about the technology and economics of the silicon chip. Many of the more esoteric terms used in the chip business are explained in the text of our book; but such passing references may not be sufficient for some readers. We therefore offer, as an optional starting-point, an appendix containing some more general information about electronics, and the semiconductor sector in particular.

Introduction

By the late 1970s the gradual realisation of the universal impact of microelectronics revived interest in many industrial and technological markets from which Britain had in effect opted out. Against this background an ambitious British Government scheme was designed to bring high-volume microelectronic circuit manufacture back to Britain – the formation of Inmos.

The United States had come to dominate the most important parts of the electronics business. In the areas where the Americans did not reign without challenge, the Japanese were busy carving themselves lucrative niche markets. But in the most important sectors the Americans had it all their own way. The world's first microprocessor, the Intel 4004, came on to the market in 1971. It was a four-bit device – that is, it could deal with data consisting of four zeros or ones at a time – and was designed to go inside a calculator.

There had been gigantic problems in developing a 10,000 transistor single chip. For them to be solved at all, let alone in just over a decade, vast amounts of money and skilled manpower had to be devoted exclusively to the project. This research was done in the United States; it took place there for the same reason that earlier American researchers had been looking at silicon as a possible replacement for germanium in transistors. The operating temperature range and switching speed of silicon components make them ideal for military applications. The political decision to devote such large sums of money and resources to a single project area was intimately bound up with the state of international relations at the time. It was the age of the cold war and the American military establishment wanted a guidance system small enough and sophisticated enough to put in the front of a Minuteman missile. The frenzied period of integrated circuit development in America in the 1960s gave its electronics industry, almost as a by-product, a lead over those in other countries that it has never quite lost.

The American electronics industry was not only provided with the funds to do all the development, but also had, in the military, a large and stable market for new products when they eventually did get to the point of production. For the first time electronics became dominated by the industry of a single country. The huge development costs involved, the structure of the economies of scale in mass-producing the chips, the guaranteed, protected markets for the products and the concentration of scientific know-how, all combined to determine that this would be the case. So by 1971 integrated circuit technology was dominated by American manufacturers, who were starting to cash in on the non-military spin-offs.

Meanwhile there had been a series of crucially important changes in radar and radio technologies in the years after 1945. As the economy of Japan was rebuilding after the war it looked for non-energy-intensive and non-materials-intensive sectors to enter (Japan is short of both energy and materials). One such industry which it was quick to enter was electronics, and in particular the commercial possibilities of the American developed transistor were quickly recognised by the Japanese. When transistor radios appeared on the mass market in the late 1950s nearly all of them were of Japanese origin. (The demilitarised economy had no incentive to build silicon transistors.) So while American industry was busy developing silicon technology the Japanese proved highly successful at making and selling low-cost consumer goods based on germanium transistors – first radios and soon afterwards television sets.

Television production started again after the war and although the first sets were baroque, valve-based monsters they soon incorporated transistorised, solid-state techniques. The screens improved too. They became bigger, brighter and flatter. The improved cathode ray tube itself was a spin-off from the war-time work on radar where improved visual displays of information were needed.

The well-known and often discussed ability of Japan to take technologies developed elsewhere and exploit them commercially had some unexpected results in the electronics industry. By the end of the 1960s, America, where almost every significant step from the valve to the integrated circuit had been invented or pioneered, saw its own domestic radio and television industries being destroyed by Japanese imports. Exactly the same thing was happening to the radio and television industries in Britain and the other countries where they were produced.

The British computer industry was going through much the same experience at that time at the hands of their American rivals, who always acquired the latest integrated circuits two or three years before anyone else and so always had the best computers for sale. American computer firms were, literally, next door to the only chip manufacturers anywhere and had close contacts with them at many levels. They also had access to the largest market in the world. For British industry it was all a very unpleasant experience. Never before had they been faced with stiff competition from superior products in their own back yards. Foresight was a commodity in rather short supply in much of the British electronics industry in the 1950s and 1960s. In the radio and television businesses, few foresaw that the development of techniques to put transistors into printed circuit boards, along with great improvements in design, would result in products far, far cheaper to produce, using a fraction of the labour and with better performance characteristics than British products. In the computer business, the firms were slow to realise that the integrated circuit was something as fundamental to the future of their industry as the valve had been to radio before the war.

In the 1970s all these factors came home to roost. The British computer industry virtually collapsed and so did the consumer electronics industry. By that time there was little they could do to save the situation. The groundwork had been done years before, when tiny Japanese transistor radios began to appear on beaches and American professors at international conferences made extravagant claims about impending revolutions in information and control. Other European countries had made similar mistakes.

Other, smaller areas of electronics were badly hit, too. Although they did not have the same mass market, process control and other electronic capital goods, the sectors which were important to the infrastructure of the economy, also found they were lagging. Process control later developed into the field of robotics.

After 1971 the focus of the electronics industry shifted towards integrated circuits and their impact began to be felt outside the area of computing. Digital circuits, those employing zeros and ones, were far cheaper to produce than analogue circuits which dominated in the days when radio was the dynamic force. Analogue circuits deal with electronic signals which are exact copies of the external signals. Before the 1970s analogue circuits were still prevalent outside the world of computers. For example, if one wanted to build a piece of equipment for industrial control, in the 1960s normal practice would have been to base its electronics on an analogue circuit. To convey pictures, sounds, numbers or any other normal type of information with a digital circuit the data must first be converted to a string of zeros and ones. This is a cumbersome process compared with the more direct analogue circuit techniques. However, because it was so cheap to mass-produce digital circuits and because they could be made so flexible — instructions can be programmed in to tell the chip how to manipulate information when it is received — it proved far more economic to go digital.

It was here that the convergence took place between the new silicon-based technology and the older communication technologies such as the telegraph or telephone. With the advent of microwave technology, large numbers of voice signals could be sent down a radio link. Analogue signals have an unpleasant tendency to become jumbled up in this environment and their separation is complicated. On the other hand, it was found that with digital chips developed for use in computers, it was possible to send, for example, 64,000 channels of voice communication up to a satellite and then decode it satisfactorily when it was bounced back to the other end of the link.

The telephone network had been built around wires designed to send the human voice. For computers to talk to each other along the public system, their digital system had first to be converted into a constantly varying wave (it sounds like a series of tones) and then converted back into digital form for the second computer to understand. In the 1970s equipment designed to transmit the human voice and to switch telephone calls (telephone exchanges) started to be made using digital techniques. The digital equipment is cheaper, can do far more things and computers can speak directly to each other. (The human voice signals are converted at either end of the link into digital signals for the telephone equipment and exchanges to deal with.)

This is why it was was important that Britain and other European countries, and to a lesser extent Japan, missed out on the integrated circuit and digital revolution of the 1960s. The powerful, cheap and flexible integrated circuits became the basis of everything it was possible to do with electronics just as the valve had been. So, computers, consumer electronics, telephony, industrial and military electronics were all profoundly affected by the integrated circuit and especially the programmable integrated circuit: the microprocessor. On top of this, many new markets sprang into life, from video games to home computers.

In 1962 the United States military was buying the bulk of the chips made; by the start of the next decade they were buying only 5 per cent. By then the commercial applications had taken precedence over military uses, the reverse of the earlier situation. Paradoxically, by 1975 it was possible to buy a space-invader game containing a more sophisticated chip than could be found in a real missile. Whole ranges of existing products found themselves being enhanced with a sprinkling of chips, from washing machines to motorcars and vacuum cleaners. Others, such as the video recorder, were only made possible for mass-market consumption through the inclusion of micro-processor controls. The growth of new markets, the complete dominance of electronics by the chip and the tightening of the stranglehold of the United States was the shape of things up to the late 1970s.

For those working in the industry, then, the environment had changed completely. The whole area had become more dominated by science and technology. In the domestic electrical industry, both because of competition from the Far East and because of automation, far fewer people were needed in assembly work. On top of this, those who were employed tended to have more and different skills. The number of components in a television set from British factories in 1972 was 1200: seven years later this had been reduced to 450, most of which no longer had to be assembled by hand. The peak of employment levels for the British industry was the late 1960s, before the impact of the changes had really been felt. Thereafter labour was shed at a dramatic rate. To take one example, for every one hundred people needed to produce an electromechanical analogue telephone exchange, five are needed for a digital model. The kinds of skills demanded by employers altered as their labour forces got smaller. Assembly workers and semi-skilled people went and were replaced by a smaller number of highly skilled designers and engineers.

The electronics industry itself experienced first the changes that were to have such a large effect on the other areas of manufacturing where its products increasingly found uses. As a general rule, it has proved a good indicator of trends in the rest of the manufacturing economy. It means fewer people doing different and more skilled jobs and a steep rise in the levels of capital intensity of the business.

The Japanese were not content with the position of unchallenged dominance in the domestic electronics industry that they had secured for themselves. In the mid-1970s through a conscious national decision, they decided to expand their embryonic integrated circuit industry. And they formulated a national plan to do for the computer and integrated circuit sectors what they had done for consumer electronics.

Britain still slept on. But not for too much longer, as we shall now see.

1 The Scene is Set

The semiconductor industry was largely invented by the Americans. By the mid-1970s, the period when the re-establishment of an indigenous, high-volume manufacturing facility was being seriously canvassed in the United Kingdom, two generations of American microchip companies had come to maturity. The American organisations had grown up in the hothouse atmosphere created on the United States economy of the 1950s and 1960s — a hothouse in which most of the heating bills had been picked up by the American taxpayer and much of the very considerable profit had gone the way of the businessmen running an industry which had expanded at breathtaking speed. In return for their money the American taxpayers had gained a very valuable national, if privately owned, asset. The country had gained a massive lead in a technology, the significance of which even some senior politicians and businessmen in other industrialised nations were only just beginning to appreciate.

This book deals with the development and the fortunes of Inmos. It is today the largest British-owned semiconductor manufacturer of high-volume, standard microelectronic components. It started life as a desperate attempt in the late 1970s to rekindle some sort of strategic presence in the field. As it was thought impossible to finance a project of this kind from the private sector, the Labour Government, through an agency for restructuring and supposedly modernising sectors considered important, was eventually persuaded to provide the necessary investment from public sources.

The agency concerned was the National Enterprise Board (NEB.) It had been given a pivotal role to play in the Government's industrial policy and was portrayed as the mechanism by which some life could be kicked into the outdated and complacent manufacturing sectors in the United Kingdom. The NEB was highly unpopular with the Conservatives, whose leadership saw it as the epitome of the interventionist approach to managing industry which it utterly despised. And it was not just the new radicals emerging in the leadership of the Conservative Party who felt a strong antagonism towards the NEB. The Heath Government had shut down its predecessor, the Industrial Reorganisation and Development Corporation, on the grounds that the tasks it performed were not compatible with a market-driven industrial base. The IRDC had in effect been resurrected after the Heath Government fell in 1973 as the NEB.

So, rightly or wrongly, any project with which the NEB was closely associated would instinctively and inevitably be seen by the political right as the poisoned fruit of an institution which was part of the foundations for a centrally planned system of the kind seen in Eastern Europe. Even the most superficial examination of the actual schemes in which the NEB became involved reveals that such an analysis owed more to myth than it did to fact. But as the left in the Labour Party wanted to use the NEB in a far more ambitious strategy of industrial intervention, such confusion was inevitable. It is worth noting that the role the NEB should or could play was as much the subject of argument and debate between the different sections of the Labour Party as it was elsewhere.

The NEB had an uphill struggle from the start to talk the Government into backing the project. It never did persuade the whole Cabinet and it was only the personal support of a small number of senior figures, including James Callaghan, the Prime Minister, that enabled it to get off the ground at all.

As we shall see, a central plank of the strategy behind Inmos was that the venture should be started with a heavy dependence on American personnel and manufacturing techniques. How far it succeeded in acting as a technology pump for the rest of

British manufacturing industry is a question to which we shall return. But it is not possible to dispute that it was planned from the start that American technology was to be the basis on which the new company would be floated. The strong association with the United States, and American nationals, was to prove an extremely contentious part of the plan in the early days. The scheme started with few friends on the left. For different reasons it had even fewer on the right. For many in Britain with a wide variety of political starting-points, the business culture, backgrounds and perceptions of those who made up the American semiconductor business were to prove difficult to understand. For some, the gap was to prove impossibly wide and they never came to terms with the Americans.

Two of the founders of Inmos were Americans who had grown up in the American microchip business. And latterly in rather different ways both had been relatively significant participants in its development. But it has to be said that the culture gap which some at least of the British experienced was a two-way street. A lifetime in the American semiconductor industry proved a bad training for coping with the culture, business methods and political institutions of Britain.

The relationships between the American industry and its Government and between the American industry and its counterpart in Britain, in so far as it had a counterpart, are of crucial importance in understanding what Inmos was set up to try to do and in understanding the relationships which developed between the individuals and organisations involved in its foundation. The story of Inmos must thus start with a rapid review of the history of the American semiconductor industry and of one particular participant in its growth, Dr Richard Petritz.

The transistor, it will be remembered, had been discovered at the laboratories of the Bell Telephone System in New Jersey in 1947 and much of the subsequent pathfinding work and nearly all of the commercial exploitation was done by large established American corporations in close conjunction with American universities. The links between the two were strengthened by a handful of hybrid academic/commercial institutions, of which Bell Labs was the largest and most successful example. Some writers see Bell Labs as crucial to the story. Certainly it and the established electrical companies were responsible for over 90 per cent of major innovations in the mid-1950s.

Later in the 1950s a pattern developed in which new electronic components developed by the large organisations were often taken up by smaller, newer firms who were mainly respnsible for their commercial exploitation and distribution. These 'spin-off firms' were typically made up of the former researchers and managers from the established companies. Such firms undertook proportionally low levels of R&D in their early years. Many argue that these 'spin-offs' were pivotal to the development of the industry, both as vital prerequisites to diffusion of the technology and as a natural consequence of a fast developing sector consistently working on the technical frontier.

By the mid-1960s, therefore, a business culture had become established in the high-technology industries of the United States which differed markedly from its counterparts elsewhere. Apart from the fact that the companies involved were dealing in techniques and products that were extremely rare elsewhere, they had also readily accepted that engineers and salesmen with an eye for the main chance would break away from their employers from time to time and set up fresh companies.

The level of public funding, particularly military funding, for research and development (R&D) was a crucial element in the development of the American semiconductor industry. According to one widely accepted source, between 1958 and 1974 the total government contribution to R&D had been $930 million, compared to $1200 million of private funds. So, an average of 44 per cent of funds were being provided from public sources.

In the mid-1960s both the desire of the United States' military to integrate the electronics guidance systems of missiles, and, in particular, its urgency over the Minuteman II project led to the consumption of vast levels of public resources. The Apollo space programme was hardly less well supported. By contrast, in the United Kingdom, total public-financed R&D in this field in 1968 was £3.6 million, only £1.6 million of which was earmarked for private firms. It was the vastly larger scale of R&D efforts in America that proved crucial.

Richard Petritz was involved in the American semiconductor industry from the start. He spent his life up to the age of 35 as a university researcher in physics. He then moved to one of the American semiconductor giants, Texas Instruments, in 1958. For ten years he worked in the TI R&D department and left just as one of the landmark technologies of the electronics age emerged from his laboratory; — Series 74 tt1, which increased the speed at which chips could operate. But despite having helped create an important branch of the bipolar semiconductor family, Petritz, along with a number of others, had the foresight to see that a completely new technology, that of metal oxide semiconductor (mos) integrated circuits, was about to have a major impact. Placed where he was, he could hardly have failed to notice.

Neither was he a stranger to financial speculation. 'I had made some investments in the stock market and found that you could make money. Investment appealed to me and I had been fortunate in getting into the ground floor of some good new issues back in the middle 1960's,' he recalls. These issues included such names as DEC and others which are now blue chips of the technology sector. 'Apart from being lucrative it taught me the value of being in at the start of one of these companies as a participant.' Petritz had also acquired some valuable stock options from Texas Instruments during his career there. He needed hardly any pushing to take the logical step of running his own business.

In the late 1960s the capital needed to start a semiconductor business was not that great. Series 74 tt1 had been developed, for example, in a laboratory employing half a dozen people using not particularly costly equipment. As, in the short term at least, there was not even the need for a new company to do research on that level of sophistication, let alone anything more complex, its costs could be kept low until it had established itself. Petritz recalled:

> I thought it would be fun to start something on my own outside the domain of a large company. Mos was a brand new technology and I could see lots of opportunities. It was already clear that the best time to start a new company was when technology was changing.

Petritz was 45 when he left TI.

He and Richard Hanschan had launched TI's tt1 range of integrated circuits between them and were astute enough to see that a large sales organisation was not necessary, at least in the early days of the company, — 'All you needed was a few decent customers.' Hanschan was marketing manager of TI. They formed a venture capital partnership, New Business Resources. The backing came from a New York firm, Wertheim, the partnership eventually being capitalised with its assistance at $7 million. The aim was to start four or five high-technology companies.

The first company to be floated by the team was Mostek, with Petritz as its first president. L.J. Sevin had worked with Petritz at TI and left in 1969 just before the company was floated. Sevin formulated the idea for a new semiconductor company and then approached Petritz as a source of capital for the project. A modified version of the original idea in time turned into the major semiconductor house specialising in advanced memory devices. It later became a somewhat troubled part of United Technologies. The half dozen engineers who formed Mostek's key resource had all worked with Petritz at TI. In early 1969 TI decided to move its laboratory from Dallas to Houston, about 250 miles further south in Texas. As the men involved did not particularly want to move, the time was perfect for them to break away.

Although Petritz was the president of the new corporation, he seems to have been predominantly an appointee of the backers; Mostek was never really his company. In any case, the original aim of NBR had been to set up a number of enterprises. The outline was to be essentially similar in each case. The people to run them would generally come out of the R&D labs. NBR was not interested in people with manufacturing experience since 'they were generally obsolete'. Petritz had good contacts within the American technical community. He was able to find NBR a regular supply of new proposals from technologists who wanted to emulate Mostek.

Quite soon the original investment of $500,000 was transformed into $30 million for the two partners and Wertheim. Although none of the other investments made by NBR became a success on the level of Mostek, Petritz managed to maintain his reputation as a competent backer of bright and lucrative technological ideas. One of NBR's companies, for example, a medical technology company called Medicis, was sold to a large corporation for around $10 million after an initial investment of only between $1 and $2 million.

Petritz was not hard up by most people's standards when he left TI. Sir Leslie Murphy, one-time chairman of the National Enteprise Board, asked him once why he kept going. Petritz replied it was because he was fascinated by the electronics business, he liked to work with young people and regarded the whole industry as a hobby as well as a way of making money. Perhaps an additional motivation for Petritz was that he had never founded and built into an industry leader a company which he regarded as his own. He seems the sort of man who would not want to settle for being a rich, comfortable success, but who had never really got into the entrepreneurial first division.

One of NBR's missed opportunities was the personal computer boom. An NBR firm had built a desk-top computer in 1973, before microprocessors were widely available or familiar. The machine sold for $15,000 and was fully programmable, but to finance the rest of the development programme the company had to be sold for $10 million in 1975 to the 3M Corporation. A few years later Apple Computer produced a personal computer which enabled it to grow into a multibillion dollar corporation. A 'truly sad' missed chance, according to Petritz.

Petritz and his partner in NBR have been credited with introducing the concept of venture management. The idea was for capitalists not simply to fund an enterprise but rather to use their experience in getting it set up and running for a limited period before handing it over to its management:

> One of the responsibilities we had was to develop managers out of the young technical people that were heading up each company. I never intended to stay at Mostek for ever but to remain President for just sufficient time for Serrif and Sevin to get the company going. I remained for some time after to liaise with Sprague which was by then the big backer. But, by the time I left, there wasn't any real role for me in Mostek, since it was properly financed and set up.

After leaving Mostek, Petritz and his wife also left Dallas for a couple of years and went up to Boston, where he performed a similar role for another of the NBR start-ups.

By 1976 Petritz appears to have become disenchanted with the kind of venture capital operation he and Hanschan had run so well. He admits to having a desire to concentrate again on working for a single company, with a long-term job. In any case he had always said that NBR was only intended from the start to have a five-year life and by then the deadline had long passed. For all the NBR start-ups he had represented the financial interests and not those of the organisations themselves. It was therefore difficult for him to go back to any of them. Besides, the successes had already grown up and flown the nest.

In the case of Mostek, for example, he had only become president in the first place, he claims, because two of the founders, L.J. Sevin and Jack Serrif could not decide between them who should have the job. 'That sometimes happens when you have two very good guys', he says. In this instance Sevin soon emerged as an heir and in the process a considerable personal animosity between him and Petritz is reputed to have developed. For whatever reason, Petritz left the scene to return to the partnership, where his first loyalty was. A return to Mostek was out of the question for him and it is unlikely he would have been welcome.

Petritz had nevertheless retained good contacts within the company. One of those he knew was a bright young engineer at Mostek: Paul Schroeder. Schroeder had arrived at Mostek in 1974, after Petritz had left, and had established himself as a star designer. Petritz explains:

> By 1977 it was as clear as the nose on your face that the very large-scale integration circuit was going to have a revolutionary effect on the semiconductor industry. Also at the same time the industry was drifting from bipolar to mos technology and I could see this would give rise to a whole new set of companies. It was going to be just like the late 1960s again.

Because the microprocessor had come on the scene since the late 1960s and because of his immediate experience in the desk-top computer business, Petritz was very tempted to try and emulate the then very young Apple Company 'and produce a rival product based on the microprocessor'. 'But, frankly, I had had enough of the end user part of the business and had a hankering to get back to mainstream semiconductors,' he recalled.

Jimmy Carter was President of the United States at the time and it was difficult to raise capital during his administration.

'The market was down and there was hardly any venture capital money around,' recalled Petritz. Venture was dead. There were hardly any semiconductor companies started between 1973 and 1978. Zilog had Exxon behind it and Synertek was backed by three other large companies. Semiconductor design and manufacture seemed to require even greater investments and therefore the resources of a large corporation to fund it. The American tax laws at the time were not generous to the private investor and there were rumours that Washington was planning to introduce even tighter regulations.

The financial institutions also had their own problems with regard to venture capital. A major law suit was working its way through the American courts, which centred around how permissible it was for responsible institutions to make high-risk investments. The final decision declared that any 'prudent investor' would stake a small proportion of managed funds on high-risk projects because the gains were so potentially large. But until the decision was handed down there was money famine in the United States for high technology. It was against this unpromising background that Petritz wanted to start a new semiconductor company.

Whilst the United States poured huge sums into electronics research in the period immediately after the Second World War and through the 1950s, to a more modest extent British achievements in science and engineering were not insignificant during the post-war years. The scale of research was smaller precisely because the economy was so much weaker but, of the resources that were available, considerable quantities were put into a whole variety of large-scale and very costly research and development plans.

It was only in the 1970s, twenty years too late, that the British establishment started seriously to question what had gone wrong. Leading British companies had in fact managed to build up at least some kind of presence in some of the very areas of microelectronics which were so obviously and glaringly absent in the 1970s. It was partly as a result of this questioning that the concept of Inmos was taken on board when it was offered, and consequently the broad details of the debate were to become of direct relevance to the eventual form of Inmos. With this in mind, it is worthwhile to take a brief look at the main elements of some of the arguments put forward and the conclusions which were widely accepted.

It certainly was accepted that the problem went far deeper than Government waking up to the need to fund vital research areas just too late to be able to do anything effective. It is arguable that some of the huge quantities of money spent in Britain in the post-war period on large and prestigious scientific projects could have been better employed in areas with more obvious and immediate applications, but really this misses the main point. It is true that until the early 1970s nuclear physics and astronomy were consuming double the resources that the Science Research Council was spending on computing, maths and natural sciences combined. But whilst observatories for radio astronomy and facilities to study the physical make-up of atomic particles do not come cheap, the amounts spent here are easily dwarfed by the sums the United Kingdom has consistently spent on research and development related to arms and the defence industries. And here it is both the absolute size of the sums involved and the effect on the surrounding industrial environment that are important. The budget for defence research and development is currently running at around £2 billion per year.

There is the strongest possible evidence that the level of commitment over many years has distorted the technology industries in a way that did not happen in the United States, and has made them less capable of responding to the very different demands of civilian R&D. According to research done by the Organisation for Economic Cooperation and Development (the figures were published in 1981), British spending on basic scientific research was lower than in West Germany, France,

Belgium or Italy, as a proportion of the overall spending on research and development. The figure for defence research and development was 58 per cent higher than any of the above countries and a bigger proportion of the total than is even the case in the United States. The Ministry of Defence itself maintains that a very high part of the overall R&D budget is spent on actual development which finds its way directly back to British companies.

But in the case of the semiconductor industry the effect during the 1960s of all of this development money was disastrous. Military parts needed to be highly reliable in order to work in extreme temperature conditions and had to be tested in many different ways with each part having large quantities of very costly paperwork following its progress. Above all, the military buyers were paying for performance and speed way beyond the needs of commercial users. The production runs for military parts are far shorter than for their commercial counterparts and the cost environment in which they are made is far more flexible. The military have never minded paying for extra performance. All these demands are very different to the ones made by the commercial semiconductor user. Here the requirement is for long runs of low-cost parts of adequate quality.

British industry found it could not inhabit both cultures and because of the multimillion pound contracts immediately on offer from the Ministry of Defence, it took the commercial decision to concentrate its efforts on military work. Despite having established a real technical advantage in the manufacture of some early standard semiconductors, companies in the area abandoned the business for all practical purposes in favour of the more profitable military business. They found it impossible to compete in the commercial markets with the relatively huge production runs and fast turn-around times demanded.

It has been argued that British companies did not try very hard to maintain a commercial, standard semiconductor base.

The technologists preferred working with the more scientifically interesting problems of improving military products on the margin and the businessmen saw a safe, secure market where the commercial risk was minimal and the returns handsome and regular.

But it is not necessary to press this point. By the early 1970s the last remnants of the British volume semiconductor industry were being closed down and the close and very profitable relationships between the Ministry of Defence and the large technology corporations were not only healthy, but increasingly taking up more and more of the country's scarce resources of skilled staff and expensive laboratory and production equipment.

2   Generation

Despite the shortage of venture capital, in the summer of 1977 the American semiconductor industry was in a confident mood. One of the most conspicuous characteristics of the market facing the community of firms manufacturing the building blocks of the new technology was its extreme volatility. The market suffered constantly from the most dramatic cyclical peaks and troughs in demand. It is a feature that remains with the business to this day. But mid–1977 was indisputably one of the 'up' periods. Demand was outstripping supply for ranges of components where the technological frontiers were moving forward very quickly.

Outside the United States, in both Germany and Japan, the gradual realisation of the massive lead that the United States had established in this crucial manufacturing sector had resulted in the speedy setting up of large government-based programmes. In Bonn and Tokyo policy-makers were doing everything within their powers to help their own industries catch up, or at least to prevent them from being left hopelessly far behind. The extent to which it was feasible to set up new non-American firms to challenge the well-established American giants was, however, still very much in doubt. Despite the desperate chip shortage of the time, it was thought that by the time any new semiconductor maker could be established, the industry could be expected to have entered the next slump. So a new entrant would inevitably need to be a relatively long-term project to stand a chance of establishing itself properly in an environment which had a tendency to become fiercely competitive in a very short time.

Many observers in Europe believed that the American

semiconductor industry had gained an unassailable lead in technology. Earlier attempts by established European companies to import this critical know-how across the Atlantic, in the form of joint-venture companies, had not been particularly successful because the objectives of the partners involved had not been identical. The American firms wanted to win a greater share of European sales whilst protecting their own home markets and giving away the minimum amount of technology; the Europeans wanted the maximum transfer of technology and access to the largest market in the world — the United States — for the product of the joint venture. No company seemed to have devised a reliable means of transferring American technology overseas, and without such a mechanism the Europeans and Japanese seemed doomed to follow the American lead forever.

Another important barrier to entry was that the scale of investments involved was, by 1977, far higher than had been required in the earlier round of semiconductor start-ups in the late 1960s. The rapid progress of chip technology demanded even more sophisticated manufacturing and design equipment, the cost of which seemed to be rising at an exponential rate. The convenient wisdom at the time was that at least £25 million (around $50 million then) would be needed to cover all the costs of entry into the mainstream semiconductor business, from the design team through to the purchase of the expensive capital equipment to the establishment of the requisite marketing organisation.

The German Government had certainly accepted the thinking behind these sums. For they went ahead and invested just that amount in Siemens in 1977, and in the process set the foundation for one of Europe's most extensive semiconductor operations. The Japanese in the end put in many times the theoretical entry figure, but spread it amongst a number of existing companies. These companies were, however, forced by the state into extensive cooperation. Those who would not agree to this condition were excluded from any participation in the scheme. A case in point was Oki.

Petritz was well aware that other countries were desperately trying to find ways of building their own stake in the integrated-circuit business, but, although well connected within the American semiconductor establishment, he lacked the high-level contacts with European governments which might have been able to provide the large investments necessary for him to realise his latest ambition.

In the summer of 1977 at a computer conference in Toronto, however, he bumped into an English academic, Iann Barron, who was to provide an entrée into British Government circles and ultimately to turn his ambition into reality in the form of Inmos. Barron was well aware of the European and Japanese Governments' desire to set up their own advanced chip makers. In the summer of 1977 he was an industrial consultant and part-time professor of Computing Science at Westfield College. But he too had been involved in the entrepeneurial end of the technology trade. In the mid-1960s he had founded a company, Computer Technology, which had proved a considerable success for a time. Computer Technology aimed at the burgeoning market for minicomputers which was beginning to take off. It started in business at about the time Digital Equipment had pioneered the market for minis. (In the inevitable rewriting of corporate histories that goes on in successful companies, DEC has emerged as though it was a minicomputer maker from the time of its foundation in 1957. In fact it was not until the launch of the PDP 8 in 1964 that it got out of the mainframe business.)

Computer Technology was unashamedly aimed at the market that DEC had identified in cheap, accessible machines for use by people who did not need a massive aftersales service department to show them how to use a computer's facilities to the full. Building on a stable customer base of research establishments, DEC went on to become a multimillion dollar giant, and, incidentally, to make a lot of money for such early investors as Petritz. Computer Technology ran into problems related to the small size of the British market and was forced to remain a small, specialist high-technology company. In the end it proved fatal, but the lessons of diversifing away from dependence on the British market remained with Barron.

The machine that Computer Technology came up with was called Modular 1. Like the 'PDP' family which DEC had engineered and sold so successfully, Modular 1 aimed to bring computers closer to the user. It was in reality an upmarket version of the PDP and predated the PDP 11 in both concepts and capabilities. According to Barron, the machine was used in some capacity in every university and government research establishment. Where DEC got around the inherent problems of accessible computing by selling each user their own computer, Modular 1 was a time-sharing machine — a revolutionary concept at the time, indeed, a concept well ahead of its time. But whilst most researchers could slip the funding for a PDP through their budget, they would find it more difficult to get approval for a Modular 1. It might have served eight people more cheaply and efficiently than eight PDPs, but the unit cost was 50 per cent higher. Another revolutionary aspect of the Modular 1 was that it contained multiple central processing units, an idea that was, regrettably, too advanced to accept.

But it was none of this that was responsible for stunting Barron's venture. The United Kingdom just did not have an industrial market large enough to support sufficient volume production to gain the economies of scale necessary to be internationally competitive. In theory, Europe offered a market comparable in size to that of the United States, but in practice the varied nations of Europe maintained their independence and were served by national suppliers. Only the United States held out the opportunity of sufficient sales to generate continuous and self-sustaining growth. American-based minicomputer-makers like Digital Equipment, for example, were able to dominate European markets as a natural consequence of their strength at home.

Few British companies had the vision or resources to take on the Americans on their home ground and so most of them, like Computer Technology, remained small specialists on the periphery of the competitive scene; this was a lesson that must have remained indelibly in Barron's mind. Although he had distanced himself from Computer Technology and became a consultant and academic in 1977, Barron was still highly respected in the field of computer design, and he was one of the few Britons in this esoteric field with recent commercial experience. It was not too surprising, therefore, that the International Federation of Information Processing Societies chose Barron to chair the plenary session of its triennial conference in 1977 on the subject of 'Computing in the Year 2000'.

It was this invitation which was to bring about the seminal meeting of Barron and Petritz in Toronto. Barron was aware of the American's track record in the chip business and had written to him inviting him to come and give his opinions of the role of semiconductors in the future of computing. But Petritz had not replied.

Despite Petritz' lack of response, the conference organising committee had, mistakenly, sent out the preliminary pro-grammes with his name listed as a panellist at the plenary session. Just before the conference started, Barron finally received a letter from Petritz saying he would attend. Apparently Petritz ignored the repeated invitations to the IFIPS event until, at another conference, he heard from a fellow speaker that his name was on the programme. Petritz then felt obliged to go after all.

As it turned out, the session was chaotic. There was an air traffic controllers' strike in Canada which started on the weekend before the conference opened. Flights could not land in Canada, and Barron's flight was diverted to Buffalo, New York. The passengers were then driven in a coach to Toronto which arrived in the early hours of the morning. Since they were supposed to arrive by airplane, the coach was not only forced to drive to the airport, so they could pass through customs, but also had to drive down the runway so they could all go in through the right entrance. The driver had, not surprisingly, difficulty finding out how to get on to the runway.

Finally the coach arrived at the conference hotel at four in the morning to further chaos. Only one of the panellists had arrived, a noted computer scientist, Edsgar Dijkstra, who insisted on playing the piano rather than discussing the content of his speech, much to Barron's annoyance. Petritz showed up just ten minutes before the sesion started. There was an audience of 3,000–4,000, despite the air traffic controllers' strike, and space was tight. The panel ended on a controversial note: Dijkstra stated that microprocessors had set back the progress of computing by ten years. After the panel members had spoken, some members of the audience fought amongst themselves to get to the microphone.

Barron recalls:

> It was all rather hectic. I hadn't slept for hours but I coped, as chairman, somehow. When it was all over we went to a very dark bar and Petritz came and sat beside me. This was the first chance I'd had to talk to him, he was on one side and his wife on the other and he leant over and said 'how would you like to start a new semiconductor company?' I took absolutely no notice, in fact, I think I went to sleep.

The two men were destined to run into each other again very soon. The circumstances of this encounter also offer a useful insight into the personalities of them both.

Barron had not intended to return directly to England after

the conference ended. Instead he had arranged to visit one of
the largest chip-makers in the world, Motorola. At Toronto
airport he was asked to explain where he was going and where
he intended to stay by the ever suspicious American
immigration officials. He had forgotten to bring the letter from
Motorola confirming his visit, and the immigration watchdogs
refused to allow him into the United States. With his casual
clothes, sandals, longish hair, thick glasses and strange (to them)
English accent, Barron's tale of dropping in to visit one of
America's industrial giants must have sounded quite implausible.

Purely by chance, Petritz was also booked on the same flight
back to his home base. Spotting Barron in difficulties, Petritz,
looking the epitome of a successful businessman, approached
the immigration desk. 'I know this guy, he's OK' was sufficient
to see Barron on to the airplane where the unlikely pair sat
together. Petritz on this occasion had a captive audience and
took the opportunity of presenting his proposal that Barron
should join him in a semiconductor venture at greater length,
and this time Barron was obliged to take Petritz and his
proposition more seriously.

Petritz's logic soon emerged during the conversation. He
already had an American engineer, Paul Schroeder, lined up to
take charge of memory products and he needed someone to
look after the microprocessor side of his proposed venture.
Barron agreed to a further meeting and a few days later the two
spent an afternoon together during which Petritz again tried to
sell the idea.

Barron did not, he says, want to work in the United States.
Petritz then suggested that if some of the money could be raised
in the United Kingdom, then Barron could have his bit of the
company in Britain. Barron said he might be able to raise some
British money and there it was left. Petritz had been through
the same routine with a number of likely partners. Lots of them
had said they could raise the capital, with little real hope.
Looked at cynically he had nothing to lose in encouraging them.

After all, an exceptional and very rich investor was required. Petritz did not believe that he could raise the sum needed from conventional American venture capital sources. The feature that distinguished Barron from the others Petritz had tried to interest in his scheme was Barron's close contacts with industrial policy-makers in the United Kingdom.

Barron had researched and prepared for various state agencies a number of reports related to British technology policy. The somewhat pessimistic tone he had taken in these reports in relation to the prospects of successfully starting a microelectronics venture from scratch in Britain, ironically, was to boost his credibility when he came to propose such a venture himself.

The timing was crucial. In the latter part of 1977 the United Kingdom, including its government, was slowly being pushed into the realisation that there was not only no real base for the manufacture of chips in the United Kingdom but failure to include them in many non-electronic products would inevitably lead to the demise of whole sections of industrial activity. Such companies as GEC had always argued that British industry could buy all the chips it needed from abroad and concentrate on integrating them into products, but this view was becoming less popular since it appeared that even a quick take-up of new technologies would do nothing to stem the decline of semi-skilled and unskilled unemployment in the manufacturing sector.

On the contrary, adoption of new technologies would, if anything, hasten the decline in many types of manufacturing jobs. Interestingly, few policy-makers or analysts argued with the direction of change, towards an economic base with more concentrated use of labour and one with fewer jobs. The arguments that there were concerned the pace of change and to what extent the creation of new sectors based on the emerging technologies would take up the slack created in other parts of the economy. The government, and the general public, had had its attention forcibly drawn to these issues by a 'Horizon' television programme, 'Now the Chips are Down', in which Barron took part.

Despite the hopes of their makers, television programmes do not often have a dramatic or identifiable impact on social and industrial policy. In most cases this is probably just as well, but this particular edition of Horizon managed to do far more than pleasantly entertain the thinking, suburban middle classes for an hour. One member of the audience was James Callaghan, the Prime Minister, and the programme seems to have alerted him to the issues at stake far more effectively than all of the background briefing documents turned out by the Cabinet Office over the preceding period of his premiership. Apart from any other considerations, the Government had little in the way of a coherent policy to combat the threat of rising levels of job scarcity which seemed to be an inevitable consequence of the advance of microelectronic-based technology.

It is important to emphasise just how fast the various fractions of the United Kingdom establishment adopted technology as an important talking-point. By mid-1978 there was hardly a trade-union official, Labour MP or middle manager in the country who was not happily pontificating about the impending revolution that was about to sweep away existing manufacturing techniques, and most industrial jobs, within just a few years.

The Government suddenly needed a plausible-sounding policy fast. And one of the sources with one on offer was the National Enterprise Board (NEB). Most of the Government probably never seriously believed that the establishment of a semiconductor supply industry would of itself create much new employment. It did, however, face an uphill task in persuading many of its supporters that this was the case.

Exactly what it was that the Government wanted to achieve we shall examine more fully later. For the moment, suffice it to say that it had rapidly become aware of the widening gap between the speed of take-up of microelectronics in the United Kingdom and the position in its industrial trading partners.

A crucial element in Barron's approach was thus that it managed to capture the spirit of the time, not only within the Labour Government itself, but also at the NEB. Set up by the Labour Government in 1975 as a mechanism for revitalising vast tracts of uncompetitive British industry, the NEB badly needed a conspicious winner.

Apart from acting as a holding company for such nationalised lame ducks as Rolls Royce, Ferranti and British Leyland, the NEB had, by various means, acquired a variety of interests in electronics-based firms but it had not established as a strategic force nor offered any dramatic solutions to the problems of the industry. The main instrument of the British state in its role as entrepreneur thus needed a dramatic gesture to fulfill the expectations of its founders.

Barron had already produced a report for the NEB which examined the minicomputer industry. The gist of the report was that investing in the UK mini industry was a waste of time and money. Instead it urged that finance should either be put upstream into the chip business or downstream into such major applications as word-processing, which were starting to grow rapidly at that time. In the course of research, one of the NEB's senior officials John Pearce, had asked Barron his opinion on what could be done about semiconductor manufacture in the UK. This was in the spring of 1977. Barron replied that he thought it was not feasible to start a chip-maker from scratch in the United Kingdom.

On his return from Texas, Barron immediately set about exploiting his contacts in the NEB. Pausing only to ask his wife if she minded him getting involved with starting another company, to which she replied 'you will do what you want to do anyway,' which he took as approval, Barron phoned the NEB. His contacts asked him to come in the very next day to talk to David Dunbar. At the end of the meeting Barron was told, somewhat to his surprise, that if he could produce an acceptable detailed written proposal and business plan, the NEB would be keen to back it. Barron explained:

> We were the first outfit to treat the NEB as a venture capital source on this scale. Up until then the NEB had been supporting existing companies; nevertheless the response of the Board, or David Dunbar at least, was highly enthusiastic and instantaneous.

Barron now explains his apparent volte-face on the feasibility of establishing a new semiconductor business in the United Kingdom in terms of the changed circumstances that the offer from Petritz represented: 'Without transfer of technology from the United States no amount of investment would have sufficed. And until I met Petritz I did not know how the technology could have been imported.'

Producing a written proposal which would convince the NEB now became the major hurdle. Baron found that he was returning to the earlier mode of communications he had had with Petritz: Barron phoning him and pestering him all the time and Petritz rarely providing the information needed. 'The fundamental problem was that Dick didn't believe a consultant from the UK could really raise $25 million. I had a credibility gap,' explained Barron.

Petritz was also busy with another project at the time. He had been hired by IBM as a consultant to compile a report based on information from manufacturers of mos memory products and was busy interviewing. As an earlier consultancy assignment, Petritz had been hired by the World Bank to advise the Government of South Korea on how to plan the development of its own electronics industry. He had recommended that the Koreans establish their own source of memory chips and prepared a plan for a company codenamed EMOS. In Korean 'E' stands for foremost. Although the proposal did not capture the imagination of the Koreans, it had convinced Petritz of the feasibility of the idea.

When Barron's persistence finally persuaded Petritz to take him seriously and start negotiations with the NEB, it was hardly surprising, therefore, that the first preliminary proposal submitted was based on the Emos document. Petritz did very litle to change the contents beyond altering the name of EMOS to KMOS. Petritz had wanted the venture to be called UKMOS, but the proposal was edited using a primitive word processor produced by one of the companies funded by Petritz's venture capital. The machine could not cope with editing more complex than the simple replacement of one character by another.

The proposal, now for KMOS, found its way across the Atlantic by late November 1977. To convince the NEB of the seriousness of his intentions, Barron submitted it without making any alterations. The proposal was obviously inadequate, however, because it proposed a relatively small company which would specialise in memory production. It said nothing about either a split between the United Kingdom and the United States in production facilities or about a microprocessor division. But it did give the NEB a concrete proposal to examine and also let them gain some insight into Petritz's idea on how the American end would be structured. The NEB team were, predictably, not entirely happy with the proposal. They wanted to establish a microprocessor company rather than one that just made memories and at £12.5 million the scale of the KMOS proposal was not exactly what they had in mind either.

Petritz joined Barron in London and in a hectic week they agreed with the NEB a larger and more ambitious programme. But there still was no actual agreed business plan. Barron was asked to prepare one. 'I knew about writing business plans, but unfortunately I didn't know very much about the semi-conductor business,' says Barron in retrospect. The discussions with the NEB had resulted in a mutual agreement that the total investment in the proposed company was to be £50 million.

This had been arrived at by the somewhat arbitrary procedure of doubling the KMOS figure of £12.5 million, to allow for the British microcomputer activities, and then doubling the amount again to allow for contingencies. 'Everyone knows such projects always cost twice as much as you expect,' said Barron.

During December Barron set about preparing a plan to justify investing £50 million. He used recent articles in the trade press to establish a central, critical expense: the acquisition of capital equipment. The plan assumed, for example, that the company would use exclusively the latest and most expensive type of semiconductor production equipment, wafer steppers. The name was new to Barron, who admits that until then he certainly had no clear idea of the function of these very costly pieces of machinery. Using published industry statistics on the average capital/labour ratio and the sales generated by a given amount of capital investment, it was a straightforward matter to calculate employment, wage costs and revenues. The rest of the details could be filled in using Barron's previous experience at Computer Technology. Some of Barron's assumptions were arbitrary but proved visionary. He included, for example, an overhead expense of 10 per cent of sales to allow for marketing costs; this was double the ratio adopted by most firms at the time but is now the industry norm.

For reasons of security and convenience, Barron even typed the proposal himself, doing much of the tedious work over the Christmas holiday. The resulting plan would not have impressed a typing tutor — it was full of typing errors — but the contents satisfied the executive of the NEB after Barron presented it on New Year's Day. The NEB executive prepared a condensed version of the plan, professionally typed, which was presented to the Board late in March 1979. It met with wholehearted approval.

Because of the size of the investment and the NEB's

proportional holding, the plan also needed Cabinet approval. Even given the mood of the time, this turned out to be tricky to obtain. There were objections from Tony Benn and other left-wingers to the entrepreneurial aspect of the plan and it was opposed by the Department of Industry, which saw the project as a direct threat to its own initiatives. But the approval was in the end forthcoming and Inmos was in business.

Despite the proposal's apparently troublefree passage through the decision-making process, the Inmos plan contained three crucial elements which were each to present the fledgeling company with massive problems in the first few years of its existence.

The first of the three 'time bombs' was the way in which the NEB's investment was given in two tranches of £25 million, the first initially and the second subject to the company making satisfactory progress. This arrangement was purely cosmetic, enabling the NEB to demonstrate its prudent handling of taxpayer's money. By the time this second instalment was to be made, the Government and the entire political climate of the nation were to be transformed beyond recognition.

Secondly, the plan assumed that Inmos would be able to borrow £15 million from normal commercial sources. This funding element was included at the insistence of the NEB, regardless of the objections of the founders. Despite the high risk involved in the venture, the NEB considered such loans to be a normal and essential part of any company's operations. The political storm at the centre of which Inmos was subsequently to find itself was eventually to render the firm's chances of borrowing £15 million negligible. It did, however, manage to negotiate equipment-leasing contracts, the leasing firms working on the principle that they could always find another home for scarce machinery.

Thirdly, there was the question of the location of Inmos's facilities. The plan assumed that the company would be free to choose, but this supposition was to turn out to be dangerously naive.

With these three time bombs ticking away internally, the new firm was also to encounter fierce external opposition from a wide variety of political and commercial sources, as the next chapter reveals.

3 Sour British Grapes

To alienate, outrage or annoy some parts of the political spectrum in a country like Britain is not difficult for any new structure or body. It is after all a conservative country, hardly a place with a heritage of coping well with rapid change in any direction and populated by a people not renowned for the ease with which they can adapt to altered circumstances, at least in peacetime. But Inmos must have set a record for the number of vested interests which it managed to line up against itself. None of the founders of the company had much, if any, experience of operation in the political arena and in any case there was little they could have done to prevent the initial reactions to the company's birth.

The price Inmos could not avoid paying for its funding by the Callaghan Government was a close identification in the minds of many with some of the Government's policies. This is not to say that some of the criticism was not based on legitimate worries about the project. Nor does it imply that Inmos, by definition, represented a force for the good, clean prosperous future, a force only opposed by the old and the unimaginative. But it is probably true to say that the management of this new enterprise were political innocents who had strong ideas about how to start and build a semiconductor company but were not expecting, or prepared to cope with, continuing barrages of political flak. And to make things worse, the flak was to come from many directions.

It was not just in the minds of the badly informed that Inmos was clearly associated with government policy. In the mid–1970s the Labour Party was not alone amongst the European political parties in power in failing to provide itself with a coherent technology policy. The small-scale industry support schemes that did exist were suddenly perceived as being inadequate to cope with the massive change in manufacturing techniques which microelectronics was threatening to precipitate. The established electronics manufacturers with interests in custom chips, Plessey, Ferranti and GEC, saw in the creation of Inmos an implied criticism of their abilities as well as a potential rival for support funds. With a few notable exceptions, their leaders were not in favour of Inmos.

The counter-argument advanced by many analysts was along the lines that Britain's existing chip-makers were structurally and temperamentally incapable of making a success of volume semiconductor manufacture. They were too large and diversified, and too tied in with the specialist military market to make the required technological and organisational innovations.

Such analyses did not go down particularly well with organisations that were anxious to portray an image to the outside world of high-technology efficiency. In addition, government funds, contracts, help and general support had been, and continued to be, a major factor in the continued profitability of the big electronics manufacturers in Britain. They were thus bound to regard a new government favourite with deep suspicion. The implicit criticism of their own judgement in eschewing mass-market chip production just made things worse. The political right instinctively felt deep hostility towards any project that had its origins within the NEB. The objections of Keith Joseph, then Shadow Industry spokesman for the Conservatives, were far more specific, but idealogically he regarded with deep misgivings any scheme coming from a body that embraced the antitheses of the free-market philosophy which he and Margaret Thatcher had been advocating with conspicuous success in the Conservative Party. The Department of Industry, at the best of times one of the most notoriously faction-ridden parts of Whitehall, had its own technology policy which many of its senior civil servants felt was put at risk by the NEB's project. The Department of Industry wanted to concentrate resources on the custom and specialist microelectronics facilities which already existed in the United Kingdom and on the encouragement of the application of the new technology. Inmos would, it felt, dilute the pool of available skilled personnel and channel money away from its more pressing requirements.

The reaction of the Department of Industry's bureaucrats to the Inmos proposal was coloured by their previous relations with Barron. In 1977 he had been a major contributor to a report on the impact of microelectronics on the British economy which had been commissioned by the Computing and Systems Engineering Requirements Board, an independent body reporting to the Department of Industry. With hindsight, it appears that the CSERB's chairman, Charles Reid, had promoted Barron's report at least partly to highlight what he felt to be the management incompetence of the Board's masters with regard to this critical area of policy. Not surprisingly, the report's contents, later published as 'The Future with Microelectronics', had not met with overwhelming official approval and the relationship between Barron and his future bosses thus got off to a sticky start.

The technology trade unions, most of whose members naturally enough were to be found in the big companies, were obviously broadly in favour of increased support to the existing fabric. So they, on this particular issue, were natural allies to both the civil servants and their employers. Employers, Department of Industry officials and unions came together in the National Economic Development Council. In particular, the sector working party dealing with electronic components had on it representatives of all three bodies and it was here that the principles of Neddy policy on this aspect of technology policy was first formulated.

Although the NEDC never regained the status and influence it had enjoyed in the first years of the Wilson administration in the mid-1960s, Neddy still was an influential organisation during the Callaghan years. Objection from this direction, with all three of its constituent parties in unison, had to be taken seriously. As things turned out, the NEDC did not get a chance to object to Inmos before the formal announcement of the scheme. Indeed, the secretive manner in which the negotiations over Inmos's formation were conducted became itself a point of contention.

Although the negotiations between Barron, Petritz and Schroeder and the NEB had been shrouded in confidentiality, leaks were inevitable. Several speculative articles appeared in national newspapers predicting some major British Government move into the mainstream of semiconductor manufacture. The idea, especially in this sketchy and unsubstantiated form, did not find universal approval. It was understandable that the NEB was keen to keep the talks quiet until the Cabinet had been able to approve the project. The concept of commercial confidentiality was more than a convenient screen. If it had been revealed in the United Kingdom that two of the founders were American citizens, a storm would have been bound to follow and the initial plans would have been damaged. Tipping off the competition in the United States would not have been a good strategy either.

Most of the objections came to a crescendo after the announcement was made on 28 July 1978. The Cabinet had approved the NEB investment on 26 May. The scheme had more than approval from the Labour Government. It was being urged ahead in a very positive way. The vice-chairman of the Conservative Industry Committee, Michael Grylls, summed up much of the feeling amongst the political opponents of the Government's industrial policy. It was totally unexcusable, he said, that the NEB should have proceeded with a plan of this kind without reference to the National Economic Development Office (a rare case of support for the tripartite body from the Conservative right). The electronic components sector working party (SWP) in particular felt snubbed. Not only had it not been consulted but the efforts that its vice-chairman, Jack Akerman, had been making in another direction were put at risk.

Akerman was managing director of Mullard, the British subsidiary of the Dutch-based multinational giant, Philips. He had been lobbying the Government to expand the small support programme that it was at the time running for the electronics industry and to widen its scope so that the British subsidiaries of foreign companies would be eligible. He felt that both this and an initiative to encourage the Government to do more to support the British television industry would be put in jeopardy by its concentration on a single company. Philips had produced some estimates of its own, predicting that a successful launch of a world superior, mass-market chip-house would require £500 million, ten times more than the £50 million sum earmarked by the Government for what was to become Inmos.

The initial secrecy had succeeded in keeping attention away from the precise nature of the scheme. Akerman claimed that he did not have the vaguest inkling of what was going on until right at the end of May 1978. Even then his information had come not from Downing Street or Whitehall, but from a reporter. But no one from the SWP actually resigned over the issue, and the NEDO secretariat was quite supportive of the idea.

The City, however, was hostile. Its major institutions smarted under the implicit criticism that they were unable to handle high-risk yet vital projects. It was easy to show that conventional financial institutions anywhere in the world had not been prepared to make cash available in large enough quantities to support a wide range of innovative activity. But the City was strongly opposed to the NEB and by implication felt the same way about its creations. Academic discussions about long-term industrial decline in the United Kingdom and the fact that financial institutions bear the responsibility of supporting, rather than making quick profits out of, the manufacturing sector have never been popular in the square mile. Inmos was widely dismissed as a peculiar abberation of socialist planning. Apart from businessmen and financiers with their noses out of joint, many informed commentators seriously doubted the sense of the United Kingdom attempting to compete in the world market for standard circuits. Indeed, this had been Barron's view a year before, and parts of the Industry Ministry were deeply opposed to the NEB's proposal, too.

Sir Keith Joseph was articulating genuine doubts when he said in a letter to the then Industry Secretary, Eric Varley, that there was scepticism in the industry as to the viability of the project 'Many informed people do not consider it prudent to attempt, at this stage, to catch up the Japanese and Americans in volume production of general purpose computer chips without multinational backing,' argued Sir Keith in a letter dated 19 June 1978. In the same letter he raises a separate issue that had already been put forward by the left. If all went according to plan, then a group of American engineers would stand to make a considerable personal fortune. 'I believe that those who take risks in creating enterprises should be able to become wealthy if they succeed. But here it is apparently the taxpayer who is carrying most of the risk.'

In fact Petritz, Barron and the small group of engineers they had already interested in the scheme had agreed to put in £15,000 each of their own money, but certainly next to the stake provided by the Government this was very small. In the Department of Industry it was pointed out by some civil servants that in Silicon Valley, after all the model for financial structures of this kind, would-be entrepreneurs were often made to stake their last penny. Perhaps a more cogent point, which neither Sir Keith nor the critics from the left made in this respect, was that if the project was a winner, then the taxpayer, as the major shareholder, stood to make by far the largest profit.

The concept of Inmos did not, however, entirely lack support from within Britain's electronics establishment. Derek Roberts, for example, who headed Plessey Microsystems, which produced high-technology, semiconductor-based products, believed that the overall increase in British microelectronics activity that Inmos would bring about could in itself hardly fail to be beneficial. Roberts was particularly in favour of combining British and American resources in a British-controlled company rather than using British cash to persuade an American company to set up a production line for standard chips in the United Kingdom. Robert's insight was particularly relevant to the strategy of his company's great rival GEC, which was later to employ him. Although GEC had abandoned high-volume chip manufacture in 1971 and concentrated on making specialist, low-volume devices since then, by 1978 it had started to realise it had perhaps made a major error.

A relatively cheap and low-risk way back into the

mainstream semiconductor business was offered by the American firm Fairchild. Fairchild had once been the giant of the chip industry and had nurtured most of the leaders of the business who had left to set up rival companies. It had prospered for years on the earnings of its early patents, but by 1978 most of these had expired and the firm was losing its grip. In particular, Fairchild had been slow to catch on to the advantages of mos technology. Expansion in Europe seemed to offer a good chance of recovery, and GEC offered to fund a joint-venture company to import Fairchild's know-how into Britain.

Negotiations between the two, fundamentally different, companies continued throughout 1978. Although the terms of the deal were never formally announced, it appeared that the cooperation between the two firms would be limited to manufacturing; design and marketing were to remain separately

'Well Sor, it wasn't here last night when I knocked off.'

within the control of each company. In terms of technology transfer, therefore, GEC was not getting a very good deal for the £20 million it was believed to be putting up to build the joint venture's factory. The closely-guarded knowledge that it was returning to the standard chip arena inevitably coloured GEC's reaction to Inmos, which it saw as a new rival for obtaining skilled staff, markets and, especially, government support, all in scarce supply.

At roughly the same time as his formal announcement of the creation of Inmos, Industry Secretary Eric Varley had launched a £70 million scheme to support British chip-makers. Although most of this cash was earmarked to aid the specialist custom circuits manufacturers, the availability of this money was the final deciding factor in luring Fairchild into the deal with GEC. It is, incidentally, ironic that Roberts was to become, a few years later, first head of research and later technical director at GEC.

The GEC–Fairchild joint venture was, however, doomed to failure. In 1979 the ailing Fairchild, ripe for takeover, was acquired by the French oil exploration company, Schlumberger, after GEC had turned down the chance of buying it with some of its several hundred-million-pound cash surplus. The French firm, which already had considerable electronics interests, quickly abandoned the venture in favour of its own European strategy.

Another strong supporter of Inmos was Ian Mackintosh, whose independent consultancy had advised several European governments on their microelectronics strategies. Mackintosh had advised the NEB and Department of Industry on the soundness of the Inmos plan. 'Everything fitted and it was a good proposal,' he said in an interview in September 1979; 'the size of funding, the people, the attitude of the NEB and the intended market were all right.' Mackintosh was also convinced that Britain needed a standard circuit manufacturing capability, and hence Inmos, because:

If you can't make them, you can't apply them and you will thus lose out in the electronics based industries of the future.
We do not need an integrated circuit industry for its own sake, but for its synergystic relationship with UK equipment manufacturers.

This, he explained, was because of the interactive and reiterative nature of chip design. New circuits were not conceived in isolation but in conjunction with the equipment makers who would eventually use them. Experimental circuits would be used to refine the design, and so on. For this process to work, both the circuit designers and the end users would have to share the same culture and, preferably, be next door to each other.

Although Mackintosh's analysis was not entirely endorsed by the Inmos founders, or at least not given much weight in the company's plans, this argument did find its adherents at the Department of Industry which, by July 1978, had woken up to the desperate need to encourage microelectronic applications. A few months before the Inmos launch, the Department announced a £15 million programme, the Microelectronics Applications Project (MAP), to offer funding to manufacturers trying to adopt electronics in the design of their products. The Department of Industry was tenaciously holding on to the project as the centrepiece of the strategy. Many officials argued that Inmos was an unnecessary irrelevance. Thanks to the arguments of Mackintosh and his supporters, the MAP scheme was seen as complementary to the NEB's funding of Inmos.

A central concept behind that funding was Inmos's ability to act as a 'technology pump' through its close contact with the established American semiconductor companies, contact that became far too close for the comfort of one particular semiconductor maker: Mostek. At least in relation to this particular company, the NEB's insistence on strict confidentiality turned out to be completely justified. Both the American founders had close links with Mostek and, as it turned out, its charismatic boss, L.J. Sevin, was to prove the fledgeling company's most formidable initial adversary.

In the period between the Cabinet's approval of the plan and the formal announcement of the formation of the company, the three founders caught the infectious mood of secrecy. Newspaper reporters were keen to find out the identity of the mystery men behind the project, which would have tipped off L.J. Sevin that he was about to lose one of his firm's most talented designers. The vital anonymity of the founders was preserved, however, more by luck than by the observation of strict security precautions. According to Barron, the London *Financial Times* was driven, in its search for the names of the founders, to assign reporters to go through all the hotel registers in the capital to find the trio. Barron recalls:

> They drew a blank because the only hotel we could get into was so downmarket it was not on their list. When we arrived, we went to the desk to book in and asked the receptionist if we could check in incognito. She shouted out very loudly to the manager: 'Here are three guys called Barron, Petritz and Schroeder who want to book in incognito.'

All attempts at such amateurish secrecy were soon rendered irrelevent by the formal announcement on 22 July. L.J. Sevin was quick to respond.

4　The Battle with Mostek

Far more than is the case with other manufacturing industries, the semiconductor business is dependent on the skills of individual designers and production experts. Chip-makers are also exceptionally reliant, especially in the American heartland of the industry, on the personal contacts of their staff to provide the principal source of new recruits. It was inevitable therefore, because of the background of its American founders, that Inmos should look at Mostek as an obvious target for its initial recruiting drive. The initial plan, all the same, did not envisage the poaching of many people.

Partly because of the personalities involved and partly because of the perspective from which Mostek viewed developments, the Inmos recruiting exercise when it did take place appeared to Mostek's executives more like blatant poaching of their staff and research activities. Within weeks of acquiring the half dozen individuals who it planned to turn into the nucleus of its design team, Inmos found itself embroiled in the intricacies of the American legal system. Mostek was granted a temporary restraining order against Inmos and the company was catapulted into a legal battle with the Dallas-based chip-house. The order covered Barron, Petritz and Schroeder personally and the design team they had started to build from former Mostek men. Inmos had, in fact, managed to upset much of the American semiconductor industry. In so far as such a group of fierce competitors could be said to have a single opinion on anything, it did not take kindly to the idea of an outside interest, the British Government, deliberately buying parts of its available technology with the expressed aim of exporting it and then competing directly against the indigenous American industry.

L.J. Sevin was running Mostek. What was more, Sevin was known to have felt that Paul Schroeder owed much of his very extensive knowledge about the semiconductor manufacturing business to his association with Mostek. Sevin discovered the plans for the launch of Inmos when Schroeder said he wanted to resign. Sevin promptly came across to London and, in what is reputed to have been an acrimonious interview with the chairman of the NEB, Sir Lesley Murphy, threatened that if the NEB invested in Inmos, then he, Sevin, would sue the company, the people in it and the NEB.

According to Barron the incident had one advantage from Inmos's point of view. It gave them some warning of Mostek's intention to go to court. It was not at the time planning to recruit many of Sevin's designers, he says, but when Petritz found out what was going on he tried to hire some more Mostek people, on the basis that if Inmos was going to be sued anyway, it might as well get something worthwhile. The suit was started by Mostek on 14 August 1978. For about a month after the imposition of the temporary restraining order none of those named could be seen to be conducting the business. Everything was meant to come to a halt.

Mostek argued that confidential information known to the defendants would fall into the hands of Inmos. It went on to maintain that such disclosures would breach contracts of confidentiality and enable the defendants to make a great deal of money for themselves at Mostek's expense. Mostek wanted the information the team had carried out with it kept out of Inmos's hands and to stop any more of its employees taking the same path. Exactly how much the preparatory activity in London was delayed it is hard to say — probably very little — but as initial developments in the States were far more crucial, problems were bound to accumulate.

It was not just the founding Inmos trio who found themselves named in the proceedings. The four engineers they had attracted from Mostek were included. David Wooten, Ward

Parkinson, Dennis Wilson and Doug Pitman all had direct experience as design engineers specialising in either mos memory circuits or microcomputer design and marketing. When the case did eventually come to court, six weeks after the granting of the restraining order, the expected and, for Inmos, feared, long drawn-out battle failed to materialise. The hearing took only a day and less than a week later the preliminary judgement was produced by the presiding judge. The judgement, fortunately for Inmos, threw out all of Mostek's claims and lifted the restraining order. 'The mere fact that Mostek claims former employees resigned to work for a company in competition with Mostek, and that this competitor will produce products that are made by Mostek and other semiconductor companies, will not justify enjoining their activities . . . ,' states the most telling passage. For Inmos its content made up for any deficiency in literary merit. Despite the clear decision in Inmos's favour, Mostek nevertheless was determined to continue its rearguard legal action. This case was to absorb a great deal of Inmos's management time and $500,000 of its funding over the following year.

It was central to the Inmos strategy that it should quickly establish itself in the mainstream chip business by in effect becoming indistinguishable from the existing American semiconductor companies. Its defence to the Mostek suit, which had been accepted by the Texan court, was that it had been behaving in exactly the way as the other chip-makers. When they wanted new design skills they went out and bought them. When they wanted to develop a new specialisation they would, if possible, poach the ideas and people needed. American employment law has been described as an appalling disgrace. In most instances employees have no security of tenure and can be dismissed with little difficulty. Advocates of free-market economics have frequently cited the resulting unhindered movement of human resources as one of the major reasons for the relative success of the American manufacturing sector in relation to its European, and particularly British, counterparts.

But the reverse implication of employees having minimal rights is that their employers are in much the same position. There is very little to stop people walking out when they feel like it and as the vast bulk of them have no formal or legally enforceable contracts, what they take in their heads they can put to any use they choose. It is a very different environment to the rather closeted scene in the United Kingdom. People change jobs frequently when they are in an expanding area or have a skill which is in demand. So Inmos's actions, whilst they might seem maverick by standards this side of the Atlantic, did not raise so much as a judicial eyebrow in America. It should also be remembered that the United States has many times more lawyers per head of the population than the United Kingdom. Litigation is thus more frequent and resorted to earlier. The legal battle with Mostek, in retrospect, was never a serious threat to the survival of the newcomer as long as its backer, the NEB, refused to be intimidated. The case did little, however, to enhance the company's reputation in the United Kingdom.

Mostek was also capable of becoming an even more potentially deadly adversary outside the courtroom and Inmos did not have to wait long before encountering the very serious problems it was to create. Having failed to win the first battle in the courts, Sevin was not about to let the matter drop. He hit on a plan both to regain the initiative and to get his staff back. The results must have seemed far more satisfactory.

At the end of October 1978, just a month after the initial hearing, but before the injunction was lifted, Ward Parkinson, Doug Pitman and Dennis Wilson left Inmos to set up their own design consultancy. Their company in time grew into one of the most conspicuously successful designers of the 64k dynamic random access memory generation of chips. The departure of the team which Petritz and Schroeder had gone to considerable trouble to secure seemed to represent a severe setback to Inmos. Although Inmos put a brave face on things, Schroeder admitted at the time that it was probably the most inconvenient time for Inmos to lose the three. One estimate made at the time suggested that Inmost had lost six months of design time and effort, and this may have been conservative.

It soon emerged that the members of the new consultancy had secured an exclusive two-year contract from their former employer but one, Mostek. 'Needless to say, we are delighted to have their services back again so soon,' gloated Charles Barker, Vice-president of Mostek. The Inmos strategy, at least as viewed from Britain, was beginning to look a little threadbare. The Ward Parkinson team represented three-quarters of the company's design team at that time, and they left in a blaze of publicity. Things were not, however, as bleak as they appeared to outside observers. One bright spot was that one of the ex-Mostek team, Dave Wooten, had decided to stay with Inmos. Despite the unfavourable reception of its first suit, Mostek had not abandoned the idea of continuing to press its case. The four designers were thus offered a substantial carrot, in the form of a lucrative design contract, but at the same time were threatened by the prospect of being named in further bothersome litigation. The three who accepted the deal were instantly attracted by the carrot, but Wooten was angered by the implied threat sufficiently to stick with his initial decision.

The defection of the trio looked particularly bad from the point of view of British observers because they remained convinced that the design and production of a 64k dynamic ram was Inmos's major goal and first priority. The loss of the three 64k dram experts thus seemed particularly damaging. This analysis was, however, based on a misconception. The Inmos business plan said that the company's first product would be a 64k dram. It also, however, emphasised that the company would make other types of memory devices, static rams (srams) and electronically erasable, programmable, read-only memories (eeproms), as well as its long-term goal of producing an innovative range of microprocessors. The logic behind the choice of the 64k dram as the pilot device was well understood by the rest of the industry. Dynamic rams have the simplest structure of any chip; they consist of a regular array of memory cells, each one formed of a simple circuit made up of a transistor and capacitor. When developing new semiconductor production processes most chip-makers would usually try them out on drams before attempting to make chips with a more complex internal structure. Drams, despite their essential simplicity, are not easy to design or manufacture, but because they are used in huge quantities in almost every kind of electronic equipment they are the highest selling type of chip and require minimal marketing.

For all these reasons, the latest size of dram, the 64k seemed the natural choice of first product for any start-up company. By July 1978, however, this perception had altered. Because of its natural attractiveness for chip-makers, the market for 64k devices, which was expected to start growing rapidly by 1980, promised to be overcrowded and fiercely competitive, especially since the Japanese industry had, in 1977, chosen the 64k dram as the spearhead of its ambitious plan to challenge the chip supremacy of the United States.

So, three months before the defection to Micron Technology of their newly acquired team the Inmos founders had shifted their priority in favour of the sram. These devices did not require external circuitry in order constantly to update (refresh) their contents. They thus required a more complex basic memory cell which took longer to design. They would cost more to produce but could be sold for far higher prices than dynamic rams. Furthermore, there seemed likely to be only one serious early competitor in the sram market, Intel, rather than dozens of forms scrabbling for a slice of the potentially much larger dram cake. 'Even if we had kept Ward Parkinson and his colleagues, we would still have gone for the 16k sram first,' said Barron many years later; 'its market promised to grow faster and it seemed, on mature reflection, the lower risk strategy.'

The setback over the defection did not seriously hinder the firm's wider recruitment activities in the United States. In particular, in October, it acquired an engineer, John Heightley, who was to prove an asset. Heightley had worked on advanced circuit design at Sandia, a United States Government-funded laboratory run under contract by Bell Laboratories. As a national centre, engineers at Sandia regularly came into contact with experts from a wide variety of American companies. Since such personal contacts were the major source of new staff in the United States, Heightley's arrival turned out to be a godsend.

By January 1979, Inmos was able to announce that, as well as Heightley, it had attracted key experts from three of its major competitors: Intel, Philips and Texas Instruments. The diversity of backgrounds possessed by these recruits was far more in line with the founders' original recruitment policy, before the personal intervention of L.J. Sevin focused their attention on Mostek. Many of the previous start-ups in the American semiconductor industry had been direct spin-offs from a single parent firm. Mostek, for example, had drawn its team almost exclusively from Texas Instruments, as Petritz was well aware.

As well as bringing with them the skills acquired during their service with the established parent firm, such spin-off teams often imported some of the weaknesses embodied in the parent's corporate culture. Right from the start Petritz in particular was keen, wherever possible, to attract talent from a wide diversity of backgrounds to form a firm with a fresh culture all of its own. Thus, ironically, the Mostek action and the subsequent defection, whilst causing significant problems in the short run, also helped Petritz achieve his longer-term goal of taking the best from the entire industry rather than a single firm. Petritz now regards the heterogeneity of backgrounds of the key company staff as a major contributing factor to the firm's eventual success.

Back in Britain, however, these complex issues were far from appreciated. As late as April 1979, a Conservative MP, Tom Arnold, was asking a junior Industry Minister in the House of Commons to confirm or deny that Inmos had not yet sorted out its product development strategy. 'Since three out of the five members of the original design team left, has there not been some confusion surrounding what Inmos will do?', added Arnold. Within a few months the questioner was to find himself no longer in opposition but as a member of the new Government. This complete reversal of political attitudes of the firm's ultimate owner was to prove just one of Inmos's worries back in its home base, as the next chapter makes clear.

5 Early Days in the United Kingdom

The two months' interval between the approval of the Inmos deal by the NEB in March 1978 and its acceptance by the Cabinet in July were spent in negotiating a formal legal agreement between Barron, Petritz and the Board. From the founders' point of view the deal that emerged was excellent. Barron, Petritz and Schroeder each obtained 60,000 ordinary shares in Inmos in exchange for their personal investments of £15,000, and they had the right to nominate other employees who between them could acquire up to 12.5 per cent of the firm's shares in future at bargain prices. The chance for the founders to make a great deal of money and key staff to have a stake in the company's success had been seen as essential to attract the American founders and the right calibre of American engineers. It was sold to the NEB as a central part of the Inmos strategy: a stimulus for the commitment and dynamism of its management. The cheap share acquisition scheme for other workers fitted neatly with the NEB's remit to promote industrial democracy: an ideological instruction from the Labour Government which had created it.

At the start of a two-year period when the embryonic chip-maker was to seem increasingly accident-prone, even its first few days of existence were to prove troublesome. In order to complete the formal deal, Barron needed to write three letters to the NEB on the letterhead of a British-based company which could be transformed into Inmos. In February he therefore acquired, through his solicitor, a shell company, registered in Bristol, called Flatprode which had a charter to trade in electronics. The first sheet of notepaper duly arrived from the printer from whom Barron's solicitor had ordered them. All

500, the minimum order, were headed 'Slatprode'. Apologising for his mistake, the solicitor duly reordered. The next batch gave the firm's name as 'Flatrode'. The final batch got it right. The cost of 1,497 wasted sheets of paper became Inmos's first overhead.

Although the American end of the project found temporary offices and began hiring staff immediately after the formal announcement of Inmos's existence, the British operation got off to a much slower start. Until the end of the year Inmos's only British facility, and its global headquarters, was located in the front room of Barron's Elizabethan farmhouse in the village of Redbourne, Hertfordshire. Barron was not, however, the sole Inmos representative in the United Kingdom. It had never been Inmos' intention to exploit the personal contacts of the founders in Britain to acquire staff in the same way as the American end of the operation was subsequently to do. But the choice of the firm's first few employees was conditioned by Barron's past experience.

As a sometime academic, Barron was a member of the Science Research Council's computing committee and chairman of that body's distributed computing project. Brian Stephens, an ex-soldier and civil engineer, had been the SRC administrator for the latter project, and he was recruited to look after the administration for Inmos. Gill Ringland, a software expert employed by the giant, London-based software house, CAP, had also worked on the project at the SRC's Rutherford Laboratory, and she was taken on as Inmos's first software manager. The firm's fourth British employee, Mike Wright, did not join until December 1978 after working out three months' notice at Plessey, during which time he was able to do a lot of work, unofficially, for his new employer. Wright had been personnel manager at Computer Technology and applied to the NEB to join Inmos. He was startled to find that he would be working with his ex-boss, Barron. Another later recruit was Peter Cavill, who worked at the Bristol design centre of the

American chip-maker, Fairchild. Cavill also made the first move. He approached the NEB in August 1978 and was finally recruited a year later.

The first priority for the tiny British team was to choose a site for the company's headquarters, find some suitable offices and move in. There was little point in hiring more staff if the only place for them to work was Barron's front room. Unfortunately for Inmos, apart from the promotion of industrial democracy, the NEB also had firm instructions to help implement the Government's regional policy which meant it was under strong pressure to persuade firms in which it had an interest to locate in areas of high unemployment in England. The Inmos business plan left the firm's location options open, stating that the management would choose sites which were most likely to aid the firm's chances of success. There was no actual commitment to locating in a development area although such a choice was described as a likely option. This was not, however, the impression gained by the outside world. 'I could have dined out for a year just by going to see all the local authorities and development corporations which were trying to woo Inmos,' recalls Barron.

Some authorities went to extraordinary lengths to try to influence the siting decision in their favour. Tyne and Wear County Council, for example, presented its case to the NEB and Eric Varley, then Industry Secretary, and held a press conference in London to curry more favour. Three local authorities and three universities in the Greater Manchester area not only lobbied the NEB and Varley but also sent a copy of their nine-page sales document to the Prime Minister, James Callaghan.

But all these strenuous efforts were to prove pointless. The British Inmos team had been busy carrying out a study of the best place to set up business and had already decided by the end of September that they wanted to go to Bristol. Inmos's own business plan favoured a location in the Thames Valley, where pleasant housing and easy road and rail access to London and Heathrow Airport had already attracted a rapidly growing nucleus of high-technology companies. The proposal had in fact suggested Maidenhead as the headquarters site and Swansea as the first factory location. Subsequent investigations forced a change of plan. Land as close to London as Maidenhead or Reading turned out to be too scarce and expensive. Looking at studies of areas where people said they wanted to move, Barron rejected Swindon and settled for Bristol. The NEB was informed of the decision as a matter of course, but the Board was under pressure from the Government. It refused its official permission and began to try to persuade Barron to change his mind.

But in November 1978, by which time Barron was increasingly frustrated by the NEB's delaying tactics and fed up with operating out of his front room, the NEB finally backed down, with some reluctance, and gave its official permission for Inmos to lease a suite of temporary offices in an unoccupied block in the centre of Bristol called Whitefriars. The NEB did, however, insist that Barron keep the office location confidential until the Labour Government could be talked round to the decision. With the NEB's approval, Inmos prepared its first classified advertisement and booked space in the national newspapers and the trade press to run it early in December.

It is clear that the NEB had still not received authorisation from the Government for the choice of Bristol by then, and so it forced the company to cancel the advertisements. In the north-eastern edition of the *Guardian*, the advert was somehow allowed to run. And it was this single advertisement that was to force the NEB's hand. Headed 'Go Inmos Young Man', the quarter-page adverts called for computer architects, software designers and engineers with experience of mos technology to apply to work at its Bristol research centre. It was an unfortunate coincidence that the first people to learn of the firm's choice were the very Tyne and Wear officials who had been trying to lure Inmos to the North East.

The premature announcement of the Bristol decision unleashed a furious storm of protest from the spurned local authorities and their parliamentary representatives. But the attraction of the production centres, then expected to employ around 4,000, going to development areas was sufficient to calm the raised tempers and by the time Eric Varley chose formally to ratify the decision, with the announcement that an Industrial Development Certificate had been granted, after intense lobbying from the NEB, MPs had left the House for the Christmas recess and the level of protest was not sustained. For Inmos it looked like a messy compromise. There was now a clear government commitment to site Inmos's factories in locations not of the firm's choosing. If the office stayed in Bristol it would have to be separated from the plants.

Even the wording of the advertisement, and the choice of Bristol, remained a minor source of embarrassment for the company for some time to come. The 'Go Inmos Young Man' slogan was attacked by the Equal Opportunities Commission as sexist, even though one-third of the firm's employees were female, and the fact that the slogan had patently been chosen to preserve a fortuitous literary allusion at the expense of precision. The Royal Institute of British Architects also got in on the Inmos attack, claiming that by a 1930 Act of Parliament the term 'architect' could only be applied to holders of qualifications approved by RIBA, which did not recognise 'computer architecture' as a valid field of specialisation.

More seriously, members representing the spurned constituencies, returning from the recess, demanded to see the study upon which the Bristol location decision had been based. A convenient leak from equally unhappy Department of Industry officials gave these MPs the ammunition they wanted. Like any piece of research work the Inmos study was vulnerable to hostile criticism, and disgruntled MPs used the standard techniques traditionally used to discredit any piece of research and dismissed its methods as incompetent and its conclusion as misleading. It was finally suggested, for example, that Bristol had been chosen simply because Inmos executives wanted to live in the Cotswolds. At Inmos they assumed that the anti-Bristol lobby was not clear on the location of the Cotswolds. Barron claims, moreover, only to have visited Bristol once before in his life. Indeed, because of intense press speculation over the first Inmos siting decision, he deliberately avoided the area until the NEB made a formal announcement of the choice.

It also went unnoticed at the time that, because of the relative decline of the British aircraft industry, traditionally one of Bristol's major employers, unemployment in the Bristol areas was higher than in at least one of the regions, Greater Manchester, that the politicians, through the NEB, were urging on him. As far as Barron was concerned, the choice of Bristol was not only commercially correct but also socially responsible.

The most serious consequence of the 'Go Inmos' incident was, however, that it exacerbated a potential source of tension between the Inmos management and their major shareholder. Although the company had been sold to the NEB as an honest business proposition which would, first and foremost, earn a handsome return on the state's investment with the added side benefits of increasing Britain's expertise in a key growth sector and improving our balance of payments, it was inevitable that the NEB, and its political masters, would seek to emphasise what for Barron was a relatively minor advance of the scheme: job creation. Barron himself must take responsibility for the estimate of 4,500 jobs which the company would create by 1984. He had derived this figure using the 1977 sales per employee ratio for the American semiconductor industry. The calculation did not anticipate the vast improvements in labour productivity that advances in process technology were to bring about. Faced by the carping of the development areas after the advertisement fiasco, the NEB seized upon the prospect of 4,500 jobs as its public relations lifeboat. The figure soon caught the imagination, which was inevitably blind to the subtle technological factors, of the local and national press. And the creation of jobs soon became identified in the public consciousness as the main purpose of the company.

This confusion was further enhanced by the additional arithmetic subtlety. The business plan called for two production units, factories, in the United Kingdom. To create the production capacity required and to allow for the smooth phasing of investment, both were to have two production lines. Thus the plan referred to four 'units' of production. The misconception that four, rather than two, factories were planned was not corrected by the NEB which was determined to hold out the biggest possible incentive to the assisted areas. From the moment Inmos's first recruitment advert appeared, the NEB and Inmos no longer appeared to be pursuing quite the same goals. The consequences of this divergence between the company's intentions and what the NEB was prepared, publicly, to say about them were later to prove debilitating for both parties. The NEB became increasingly entrapped by its public posture. There was also a growing gulf between Inmos's plans and intentions and what was reported in the newspapers.

The NEB was determined that the plans, intentions and internal decision-making of its protege should not be revealed to its commercial rivals, an attitude which produced suspicion from the beginning. The NEB imposed a cloak of confidentiality, described by Barron in an early interview as 'paranoid', that helped to sour Inmos's relations with the British press sufficiently for them to remain appalling for the next few years. The climate of misunderstanding produced by the NEB's attitude was most pronounced in relation to the firm's product development plans. The press had become convinced, as a result of an early, accurate, leak of the business plan, that the first Inmos device was to be the 64k dram, then tipped to become the best-selling chip in the next few years.

The plan did, indeed, state that Inmos would produce a 64k dram as its first target. But, by the time a multitude of press articles were questioning the wisdom of this target because of the intensifying competition from such established American chip-makers as Texas Instruments and Mostek, the founding trio had already, as explained in the last chapter, changed its collective mind. The Inmos management team were prevented by the strict NEB embargo from doing more than giving strong hints at this change of heart, which the press in general did not pick up. At the first Inmos press conference, for example, a company spokesman said over and over again that the first product was not going to be 64k dram, but this was never reported.

Yet despite the popular doubts and misconceptions over the company's prospects and the petty quibbling over the wording of its advertisement, the reaction of Britain's technical community turned out to be almost inconveniently enthusiastic.

The 'Go Inmos' advert had never been intended as an attempt to poach experts from Britain's few sources of semiconductor expertise. The business plan gave a solemn undertaking that the company would not exacerbate the chronic shortage of such critical skills and promised that recruitment would come mainly from fresh graduates. In any case, engineers with the particular skills Inmos needed for its British operation in microprocessor design were virtually non-existent in the United Kingdom; the development of them was one of the main reasons for setting up Inmos in the first place. It therefore came as somewhat of a surprise to Barron and his tiny staff that the official appearance of the firm's first recruitment advert in February 1979 generated an overwhelming response. 'About two-thirds of the engineers employed in the UK semiconductor industry replied,' said Barron, 'and the four of us had terrible trouble just coping with the 1,000 applications. We all took piles of the curriculum vitae home with us every evening and sorted them into priority, we then started interviewing from the top of the pile downwards.' Although the British team did not engage in the kind of intensive head-hunting through personal contacts that the American founders found effective, at least four of the new recruits had links with the SRC-distributed computing project with which the first three Inmos staff in the United Kingdom had been associated. The University of Warwick, in particular, provided the nucleus of what was to grow into Inmos's processor design team.

It was during this phase of the recruitment process that the most momentous single event in the entire Inmos saga was to occur. For a while at least it did not seem particularly significant to them: the May 1979 General Election. But for one director of the company, the ominous significance of the Conservative victory was immediately evident. David Dunbar, the senior executive of the NEB, whose initial enthusiasm had done much to get the project off the ground and who had subsequently been appointed to the company's board, was

travelling back from a meeting with the firm's American directors accompanied by Barron on the day of the election. The pilot picked up the election result on the radio and relayed it to the plane's passengers. According to Barron, Dunbar turned to him and said: 'we might as well stay on the 'plane and go back to the States'. Dunbar's reaction, prompted by his greater political sensitivity, was to prove accurate. That September he was to resign from the NEB and Inmos to take up a senior management job in the private sector.

Barron, however, was less concerned about the change of political complexion of his ultimate bosses. 'We noted that the Tory Government was starting to make negative remarks about the company and its prospects, but we took no notice until the entire board of the NEB resigned later that year, in November,' recalled Barron. One new recruit who resigned to join Inmos just after the election was told by his previous firm's chairman, who had just been to see the new Industry Secretary, Sir Keith Joseph, 'you ought to stay here, Sir Keith said he will close the place down'. But this apparently was an isolated incident, as the company's next recruiting exercise demonstrated.

As promised in the business plan, Inmos intended to hire a lot of fresh graduates. In the summer of 1979, therefore, the firm wrote to the major universities to offer a 'once only' chance for graduates to join Britain's first contender in the standard chip business. The response, as it had been to the 'Go Inmos' advert, was almost embarrassingly enthusiastic. There were far too many top-quality applicants for the tiny Inmos team to interview individually. 'We took them all to a hotel for a weekend,' explained Barron, 'and spent a lot of time drinking and talking to them. We chose the ones we liked who could still stand up at the end of each evening.' Some, it should be added, were teetotal. In the end the company got far more new graduates than it had originally intended. 'We made offers to 16, thinking a 50 per cent hit rate would be good, and

15 accepted.' Even the one who did not accept asked if he could join a year later after studying with Carver Mead, a noted chip design expert, in California. So when the graduates joined the company in August, they totally outnumbered the rest of the staff.

The British team also got involved with the task of helping the American operation, which was keen to get into production as quickly as possible, with the selection and purchasing of manufacturing equipment. Inmos had established an understanding with the NEB that, providing the performance and price were acceptable, it would buy its expensive plant in Britain. Unfortunately, however, as a natural consequence of its lack of indigenous high-volume chip manufacture, British makers of semiconductor production equipment were thin on the ground. One British participant in this specialised business was Lintott Engineering, which had been set up by scientists from the Atomic Energy Authority's labs at Harwell, near Oxford. Lintott made ion implantation machines, which were used to shoot highly charged particles of obscure elements into the silicon wafers on which the chips were formed.

An Inmos team spent a lot of time looking at a Lintott machine which it had acquired and shipped to the United States. Eventually it was forced to conclude, however, that, in common with much British high-technology equipment, the Lintott implanter was technically very good but not sufficiently robust and practical for use in a working factory, and the machine was returned to the makers. At one demonstration the machine broke all the wafers and water was flowing out while hundreds of thousands of volt electrical discharges sparked around the room. Inmos ended up buying ion implanters in the United States, and Lintott was itself acquired by a Californian equipment-maker shortly after. Inmos also investigated the possibility of buying some of its masks, used to define the patterns on chips, from Harwell's sister laboratory, the Rutherford, where it made them using high-energy beams of electrons to draw the circuit configurations. Most such purchases were eventually made, however, in the United States.

The only significant purchase of British production equipment that Inmos made was of plasma-etching machinery from Electrotec, a firm also based in Bristol. Using high-energy streams of plasma (a completely ionised gas consisting of electrons and atomic nuclei) to strip away unwanted layers of material from silicon wafers during processing was then a relatively novel process. It proved to be, however, far more efficient than the wet chemical-based methods previously used. Although the Electrotec machine was not perfect, it was judged by Inmos to be the most advanced equipment then available for metal etching. 'It turned out to be a material factor in the success of our aggressive strategy of using only the most advanced process technology,' commented Barron.

The NEB was undoubtedly unhappy about Inmos's failure to buy very much of its equipment in Britain, but soon, however, Inmos was to discover another, more contentious, source of disagreement with its majority shareholder: the choice of location for its first factory. Barron and Petritz were convinced that the advantages of locating its factory next to its development centre were considerable. At Mostek, Petritz had observed how designers had 'walked down the corridor' to chat with the production people about the progress of their devices. The argument for a close proximity between design and production was a microcosm of that used by Mackintosh to justify the establishment of the company in the first place. After the furore over its first location decision, in January, the Inmos management had thought it wise to commission a study from an independent body to recommend where the firm should put its production facilities. This was to a large extent conceived as a purely cosmetic exercise designed to shield the company, and the NEB, from the political opprobrium that was inevitable whatever area was finally chosen.

The NEB concurred with this course of action and was

persuaded by the company to bear a share of the cost of retaining PA Management Consultants to carry out the study. PA was therefore commissioned in January to consider the best location for the Inmos production sites 'with the firm intention of locating them in an assisted area . . . [and] also [to] study where the official headquarters of Inmos should be located'. The latter part of the brief appears, incidentally, to have been added by the NEB. The distinction between 'technology centre' and 'headquarters' had never been taken seriously by the company (Inmos's international headquarters was still Whitefriars six years later), although it had proved face-saving for the NEB and the Prime Minister, James Callaghan, during the earlier row over the Bristol choice.

The PA study results were expected in May, but did not arrive until August. As expected, the PA report named Bristol as the best place for the first of Inmos's factories and the NEB was informed this was also the Inmos board's choice soon after the report was delivered. Nevertheless, when preparing the NEB's annual report accounts in the autumn, the NEB's boss, Sir Leslie Murphy, insisted that the report should include a statement that would be interpreted by a casual reader as a commitment that the first British plan would be sited in a development area. Barron, in turn, insisted that Sir Leslie should edit out what he described as 'these weasel words'; but, onimously, the weasel words stayed in. According to Barron, PA Consultants were highly sympathetic to Inmos's plight. Like Barron, the consultants were convinced that a site in the North would be commercially unacceptable, so they had 'reworked' the figures to show that a factory in Cardiff, South Wales, which was in the nearest development area to Bristol, would be the next best thing.

Inmos never had a chance, however, to take this clash of wills to a mutually agreed conclusion; the entire NEB board resigned, in November, over a disagreement with the Government which had little to do with Inmos. The Inmos management was quick to respond. As soon as the new board had got its feet under its desks, Inmos made a presentation of the firm's progress and its case for Bristol. The new board, under the chairmanship of Sir Arthur Knight, much to the distress of the Conservative right, came round to supporting the Inmos cause in remarkably quick time. It was a change of heart that was to affect a series of Thatcher appointees and to which we shall return. The board agreed that Inmos should be granted its second tranche of funding and endorsed its decision to locate its first British factory in Bristol.

The NEB quickly relayed its decision to the Department of Industry, expecting that it would promptly be approved. Just six days after the decisive meeting on 21 December, the company announced publicly that it had received approval for its second £25 million investment and that its first British factory was to be in Bristol. The Inmos management team was delighted at the prompt and favourable decision it had extracted from the NEB. Barron, in particular, had suspected

'Yes, Minister, I think I know what is expected of me.'

that Sir Arthur had been appointed specifically by Sir Keith Joseph to run down the NEB's involvement in high-risk, high-technology ventures. In press interviews soon after his appointment, however, Sir Arthur stated that he favoured the NEB continuing to act as a merchant banker to fund high-technology ventures that Britain's conventional financial institutions refused to consider.

His deputy, Sir John King, however, had described the NEB's diverse holdings, in electronics start-ups, such ailing giants as British Leyland, and established firms on the mend like ICL, as 'an absurd hotchpotch'. He opined that the NEB should not extend its venture capital activities but should instead concentrate on providing first aid and treatment for industrial casualties. Another appointee to the NEB who might reasonably have been considered likely to be hostile to Inmos was Sir Robert Clayton, who was also technical director of the giant GEC and chairman of its chip-making joint venture with Fairchild.

Although Sir Robert had presided over the abandonment of high-volume chip manufacture by the GEC in 1971, he had more recently become a fervent supporter of Britain's need to regain a stake in the standard chip business. As a key executive in one of Inmos' likely competitors, however, many thought it unlikely that, no matter how hard he tried, Sir Robert would be able to make completely objective decisions about Inmos' future. As it turned out, Sir Robert's conflict of interests was never to become a serious problem for Inmos. But its determination to combine its factory with its technology centre in Bristol was to prove infinitely more troublesome.

It was always expected that the United States' operations would get off to a quicker start than those in the United Kingdom and, despite the temporary setback created by the Mostek law suit, this is certainly what happened. The business plan called for the Inmos operation in the United States to recruit a research and development group to design memory chips and develop the processes for making them. It also gave the American team, under the leadership of Petritz and Schroeder, the job of setting up a prototype production-line to enable the company to bring its products to market in the shortest possible time.

The first task in the United States, as in Britain, was recruitment. By January 1979, Petritz, then managing director of the company, was able to announce some spectacular appointments at the fledgeling firm, which to some extent made up for the Micron Technology setback. Apart from Heightley, who with Schroeder played a valuable role in the head-hunting exercise, perhaps the most significant new employee was Thomas Hartman, who had previously been running Intel's most advanced wafer fabrication plant in Portland, Oregon. Hartman was to take responsibility for establishing production facilities on both sides of the Atlantic and also oversee all assembly, test, planning and engineering functions. It was quite a coup to have lured away such a key man from one of Inmos's most potentially important rivals.

A Swiss, Dr Fred Gnadinger, was recruited to look after process development. He had previously been head of R&D for Faselec, the Zurich-based subsidiary of the Dutch electronics multinational, Philips. Like Schroeder and Heightley, Gnadinger had learned his trade at Bell Labs. Heightley's memory products development team was strengthend by the defection, in January 1979, of Shef Eaton from Mostek. Eaton was to lead the team that was to design the Inmos 64k dynamic ram. Kim Hardee had also joined Heightley's team that month from Harris Semiconductor with Rahul Sud, an Indian, who was to join the company later from Signetics, Hardee went on to design the chip most responsible for the firm's survival and ultimate prosperity: the 16k static ram.

Simultaneously with the announcement of the new appointments, the American operation also made public its decision to establish itself in the town of Colorado Springs in the mountainous State of Colorado. Inmos's first American location had been a suite of temporary offices in an unsalubrious suburb of Dallas, Texas. Petritz and Schroeder had spent the latter half of 1978, when not working on the defence of the Mostek suit, looking for a suitable geographical base. Both had ruled out Silicon Valley in Northern California, since the concentration of semiconductor makers there, although a considerable attraction, had already created a local manufacturing labour shortage and had dramatically raised the cost of living for skilled staff. Intel, for example, had located its latest plant out of the Valley in Oregon. Schroeder was keen to set up in the Boston Area (he had been educated at the Massachusetts Institute of Technology), whereas Petritz was quite happy in Texas and did not want to return to the North East where he had already spent two years running one of the firms supported by his venture-capital outfit.

As a compromise they looked at Denver and Colorado Springs, in Colorado, at Phoenix, Arizona, where the industry's second largest company, Motorola, is located and at the Research Triangle Park in North Carolina in the 'sunbelt' which was at that time attracting a variety of high-technology companies. Their first choice was Denver, and they tried to acquire a site in Evergreen, a suburb, but the deal fell through and they fell back on their second choice, Cororado Springs, in

December 1978. Schroeder had been particularly keen on the final choice because he had already viewed the area some time earlier when Mostek first considered moving there. The ultimate choice of location in the United States was, coincidentally, similar in character to that made at about the same time in Britain. Both Bristol and Colorado Springs were the sort of place engineers wanted to move to; in the case of the latter it is where many Americans dream of taking backpacking and skiing holidays. So Inmos' recruits in the United States first went to work in rented offices in Colorado Springs, and soon those offices were bustling. Once someone had been persuaded to join, usually over the telephone, they would often be at work in Colorado the very next week.

Although the choice of company location in the United States had not been surrounded by the high-level political flak associated with Barron's decision to set up in Bristol, the NEB inevitably became involved in the American operation's next major decision: the planning of its production facilities. There was some disagreement among the American executives over the best strategy. One option was to build a new plant from scratch, ideal in the long run, but extremely time-consuming and expensive. The second option was to acquire an existing new building and make it suitable for wafer fabrication. Thirdly, there was a chance for the company to take over an old building a few miles from Colorado Springs, in Fountain. This was originally a gun factory but had been converted by DEC to make disc drives. This could be adapted to chip production with relative ease.

The debate became fairly heated. At stake was not only the style and strategy of the American operation but also the crucial point of how much of the initial NEB investment of £25 million should be spent outside Britain. The NEB chairman, Sir Leslie Murphy, insisted upon playing a major part in the decision-making. In the end a compromise was hammered out. A small, temporary, line would be set up in an existing building in Harrison Park and a 54-acre site was acquired nearby at Cheyenne Mountain on which the company would build a brand new facility, a showplace.

The new plant was to have an ultimate capacity of 360,000 sq.ft. of which 120,000 sq.ft. would be built at first with an initial 20,000 sq.ft. clean room (the heart of the factory where the chips are actually made). That decision was taken with the reluctant approval of Sir Leslie, in August but was not widely publicised at the time. The implications of this decision were to be profound; it altered the whole shape of the company and is something to which we shall return. It also represented the first, potentially politically embarassing, divergence from the original plan endorsed by the NEB. The Cheyenne Mountain building was obviously going to be much larger than was needed for a 'pilot' or 'prototype' production facility: it was to be a full-blown manufacturing plant, the first the firm was going to have, and it was not in the United Kingdom.

One argument used to justify the building of a beautiful 'palace in the desert' was commercial. In order that Inmos would be able to attract staff and eventually customers in the largest chip market in the world, it had to have a high profile in the United States. Schroeder had been a particularly firm advocate of this philosophy and Petritz supported the idea of having a single building large enough to contain all of the firm's diverse functional groups under a single roof.

The second argument, although somewhat specious, was nevertheless the one that ultimately convinced Sir Leslie, was technical. The American chip experts argued that the minimum capacity for a prototype facility was 1,500 wafers per week using a single shift of workers. Harrison Park was only large enough to contain one piece of each type of equipment necessary on the production-line, so if any one machine went wrong the whole line stopped working. Cheyenne Mountain thus had to be larger and have duplicated equipment in order to be able to guarantee the right level of production. Although Sir

Leslie had been convinced of the need for the company to make a big, expensive splash in the United States, the decision was by no means unanimous. Both Hartman and Barron, in particular, disagreed. Hartman felt that the firm's limited resources should best be spent on essential product and process development, and that the beautiful buildings could wait until the company was well established and earning money. Finding himself basically at odds with the rest of the American management, Hartman resigned and went back to Intel.

Barron was fundamentally concerned over the whole direction the company was taking and he, too, tendered his resignation. He recalled:

I did not think a 120,000 sq.ft. facility in the Rockies with a capacity for 5,000 wafers a week was in accord with the basic principles of the company. The plans for Cheyenne Mountain dramatically changed the intended ratio of investment between the US and Britain.

The American end of Inmos seemed to be getting strong at the expense of the British end. Later Barron was to say that he seriously started to doubt the extent to which his American partners were committed to establishing a viable manufacturing facility in Britain. Sir Leslie did not accept Barron's resignation. As the only high-level Briton in a British-owned company, Barron's presence was considered vital. Sir Leslie told Barron that he understood the reasons for his disquiet and that, in time, he would revise the management structure to ensure a better balance between the British and American operations. Barron allowed himself to be persuaded. 'I gave in because I thought by letting Paul have his way, he would be less obstructive to the UK activities, which I judged was worth it,' he remembered. In the event, Sir Leslie and the rest of the NEB were not to stay around long enough to make good the promise to Barron. They resigned in November, and it was not until a year and a half later that any real management changes were made. In the meantime Barron was bitterly disappointed by Hartman's departure. But by arguing with the American founders he had tarnished his image and they were not too upset to see him go.

August did also, however, herald some good news for Inmos. Its long, drawn-out legal wrangle with Mostek was finally settled. The case was scheduled to be heard on 20 August but, given the fact that the preliminary hearing had found totally in Inmos's favour and that three of the five ex-Mostek designers had since defected to form Micron Technology with Mostek's connivance, it was deemed unlikely ever to come to trial. In fact, an out-of-court settlement was arranged which prevented Mostek from bringing any further actions in support of the majority of its complaints. The details of this settlement have never been made public. Inmos might have been caused a lot of trouble and inconvenience but at least now they were free from the suit.

Hartman was never replaced, but Ralph Bohannon was lured away from running Texas Instrument's most advanced chip-development plant in Houston, to be Inmos's American manufacturing manager. It was not the first time that Petritz and Bohannon were to find themselves working together. Petritz had hired Bohannon into TI in the mid-1960s. Bohannon, in turn, recruited another ex-TI man for Inmos, John Perry, as engineering manager. Immediately prior to joining Inmos, Perry had been working at Motorola's chip-plant in East Kilbride, Scotland. So, despite the loss of Hartman, the Colorado Springs operation was making progress by the end of 1979. Construction work had been started on Cheyenne Mountain in October and the Harrison Park prototype plant was well on schedule. In January, Petritz had predicted that pilot production would begin by the end of the year and, somewhat uncharacteristically for the chip business, that prediction was actually fulfilled. Another of Petritz's forecasts, that the first shipments of products to customers would start early in 1980, was not, as we shall learn later, to prove so accurate.

One of the reasons that Inmos was able to start processing silicon so rapidly was that it did not face the problem of buying production equipment that fitted with its existing machinery, a difficulty that confronts all established semiconductor makers. Despite the fact that the chip boom was still at its height, Inmos had no trouble getting hold of production machinery. Here it was helped by its early commitment to using only the most advanced production technologies. The newest machines were less in demand than the more established types of process plant.

Seen from Colorado Springs, 1980 seemed to offer nothing less than another year of steady progress. In particular, the Conservative election victory in May had gone almost unnoticed. The company still seemed convinced that all it had to do to get the second £25 million investment from the NEB was to demonstrate satisfactory progress on implementing the business plan. The American management team also felt, somewhat naively, that the accession of a Conservative Government would give them more freedom of action. 'We had heard the Conservatives did not believe in state intervention in industry', said Petritz, 'and we thought they would therefore allow us to make such major decisions as the choice of UK plant location without interference'. Inmos quickly started a major campaign to talk the new NEB board into allowing it to locate the plant where it wanted. They feared that waiting until the new board had settled in could delay the funding and location decisions by a further twelve months. The company was therefore pleasantly surprised when the NEB made a very quick decision in its favour. It seemed unlikely that the new Industry Secretary, Sir Keith Joseph, would veto the decision of the board he had just installed, and that a quick public announcement would 'steamroller it through the Cabinet'.

Petritz was thus confident that the Conservatives would soon give the go ahead to the next phase of the company's development. This confidence was partly based on his view of what course of action was in the Government's best interests. Up until then it had spent the first £25 million of British funding on an almost exclusively American semiconductor operation; if it wanted the British end to catch up it would have to move fast. The Government was not to share this view of the rational course to take; nor was 1980 to prove a year of steady progress for the young company but rather one of considerable trauma.

7 Second Thoughts

In retrospect, the Inmos founders recognised that persuading the NEB to announce both the endorsement of their second £25 million of planned funding and the choice of Bristol for the first factory site at the same time had been a major tactical error. By the time Sir Keith Joseph had had a chance to consider the NEB recommendations several months had passed and he had plenty of time for second thoughts. Petritz and Barron are still convinced that if the decision had been Sir Keith's alone to make, their tactics would have succeeded. Sir Keith is known to have become quite positive about the company's prospects. Petritz maintained that the Conservative minister had no objection to Bristol as a factory site. But all of the development areas seem to have applied some very effective pressure designed to force the factory away from Bristol.

The first public manifestation of the kind of pressure Sir Keith was to face came when, early in January, Alan Williams, Labour MP for Swansea West and former Industry Minister, attacked the choice of Bristol as 'a betrayal of a firm and clear commitment on behalf of the board of Inmos', made to him while he was in office, to locate the factory in an assisted area. Williams was one of the few MPs who, during the Christmas recess, had noticed the Inmos announcement. He had wasted no time in writing to the NEB to demand an explanation for what he regarded as an extraordinary act of treachery. The NEB's deputy chairman, Sir John King, wrote in reply that the NEB had reviewed the recommendations presented by Inmos at a meeting on 21 December and concluded after 'long and involved discussions . . . that it did not seek to force Inmos into a commitment that it did not wish to make'. The letter went on to say that the Inmos board had stated that the firm's second factory would be in an assisted area. Sir John apologised if this decision was contrary to promises made to Williams while he was a minister but no attempt was made by Sir John to deny that such promises had been made. Barron was, of course, quick to deny that any such commitment to locate in a development area had ever been given by Inmos.

Angered by Barron's denial and by the contents of the NEB's letter, Williams promised to mobilise the groups of Labour MPs representing the various assisted areas rejected by Inmos to protest the choice in the House of Commons. In support of the claim that the company had broken its word, Williams quoted the NEB annual report for 1978 which stated: 'The firm intention is that the United Kingdom production facilities will be located in assisted areas'. He also asserted that he had, over a year earlier, three times refused an industrial development certificate for Inmos's technology centre in Bristol until the company undertook formally to locate the factories in assisted areas. On the first point Barron was able to state categorically that the 'weasel words' were those of the NEB and not of the company. In connection with the second claim, it is evident that Williams's memory is again at odds with Barron's.

There was considerable turmoil over the granting of an industrial development certificate for the technology centre — so much confusion, in fact, that the Bristol office of the Department of Industry was forced to process the applications in just three hours in time for a ministerial announcement. The vetting of Inmos's application was not therefore as thorough as that applied in normal circumstances, especially as the Bristol bureaucrats had not been given advance warning by Whitehall of the need for urgency. Barron had completed the industrial development certificate application in a rush and had, as well as the plans for the technology centre, included a specification for a Bristol factory. Both were approved. So throughout 1979 and during the subsequent furore, Inmos possessed, by bureaucratic accident, an official document permitting it to build a factory in Bristol. In any case, the question of whether Inmos had ever given a commitment to locate its first factory in a depressed area was never publically resolved.

While the Inmos team was still quietly confident that, despite the fuss being created by various Labour MPs, Sir Keith would nevertheless endorse the NEB's approval, at least one minor source of uncertainty over the firm's future was removed. In the middle of January Sir Robert Clayton resigned as chairman of GEC–Fairchild. Ever since Fairchild had been acquired by the French oil services group, Schlumberger, in September 1979, doubts had been growing over the future of its joint venture with GEC. It seemed unlikely that the French-based multinational, which was keenly diversifying into electronics, would want to be involved in a partnership with a British firm of comparable size. These doubts were fuelled further when Wilf Corrigan, who as president and chief executive of Fairchild had been the architect of GEC–Fairchild, resigned a few months later. Along with Sir Robert, David Marriot, managing director of the joint venture, also announced that he was leaving. Although Sir Robert's departure must have eased Inmos's anxieties over his ability to cope with such explicitly divided loyalties, his move, and that of Marriot, convinced most observers that the GEC–Fairchild deal was clearly in bad shape, leaving Inmos as the sole serious contender in the race to re-establish a Brish-owned supplier of commodity integrated circuits.

Speculation over the venture's imminent demise were not dispelled by such statements as 'to read any such supposition into the resignation would be premature', which was made at the time by a Fairchild spokesman.

According to Petritz, it was not until the end of February that he started to worry that there might be serious problems over getting Government approval for the new factory and the money to build it. On 18 February he commented: 'As far as I

know the thing is going smoothly towards getting the final commitment in the UK.' But if approval were to be delayed much beyond the end of February, he added: 'it could affect our ability to get production in the proper time span in the UK.' At the same time Barron described the delay as 'frustrating' and stated his doubts that production could ever catch up with the firm's original schedule. He was worried that the delay could have serious consequences for the company, in terms of loss of output (worth, he estimated one-third of a million pounds per day) and markets.

By March they were starting to get seriously worried about the delay in approval and did not know what to do next. The one thing the management team was forced to do was to attend a lot of meetings. Throughout March and April there were continuing discussions on funding and location. Barron recalled:

We had a number of meetings with Sir Keith and we gained the impression he was broadly supportive personally. He was not, however, prepared to take the decision on his own and wanted the Cabinet to agree since his conscience told him the issue went beyond his personal competence and ministerial remit.

Thus he, Petritz and Schroeder became involved in a range of discussions with a wide variety of politicians. In April, for example, Barron and Sir Arthur Knight went to a meeting of the economic advisory committee of the Cabinet. Barron recalled that at least two of the ministers, John Biffen (Treasury) and David Howell (Environment), were hostile to making any further investment in Inmos, and the Scottish and Welsh Secretaries, Nicholas Edwards and George Younger, were determined to see the plant in a development area, or else. Barron had great difficulty articulating just why it was necessary to have the factory and the technology centre so close together. He was sufficiently indiscreet to say he wanted the manufacturing and design teams to be able to meet in the pub after work to discuss progress. Barron was immediately aware that he had not made a good impression. A story circulated later to the effect that, the Prime Minister, Mrs Thatcher, had been told that the only reason Inmos wanted its factory in Bristol was so the staff could drink in the pub of an evening.

Despite their involvement in seemingly endless discussions, the Inmos management were getting very little feedback on how their case was progressing. If the firm itself felt that it was being kept in the dark, however, this feeling was even more prevalent among the journalists who were trying to cover the Inmos story. Throughout the first six months of 1980, newspaper reports appeared regularly, saying first that an Inmos decision was expected 'soon', then 'within a few days', next that it had been 'delayed', and so on, to the increasing frustration of the press and annoyance of its readers. Two fairly long-lasting effects thus survived from this period. First, relations between Inmos and the press, already imperfect, deteriorated still further. Secondly, the general public acquired an ingrained scepticism about the workings of the company, at least in relation to what it read about them in the newspapers.

Despite the dearth of hard facts about Inmos's future available to reporters, however, there was one development in April about which the press seemed better informed than the company. Sir Arnold (now Lord) Weinstock, chairman of GEC, had approached the NEB with a view to taking Inmos off its hands. This was a clear signal that Fairchild had finally pulled out of the GEC–Fairchild deal, although there was speculation at the time that GEC saw Inmos as a complement to, rather than a replacement for, the joint venture because of Inmos's strengths in mos technology. Although the NEB and Sir Keith must have been delighted that the private sector, in the form of Sir Arnold, had finally taken an interest in the state's risky chip venture, it was unlikely that the Inmos management would have welcomed the move, even if it had been formally told of it. The contrast between Inmos' ambitious entrepreneurial style and Sir Arnold's obsession with short-term profitability would inevitably have caused problems. But, as it happened, negotiations never got off the ground; they were initially hampered by the need to protect Inmos's commercial secrets from a potential competitor and when Sir Arnold and his representative on the NEB, Sir Robert, finally got their hands on the business plan in May, they decided that the investment was not for them. Barron remained convinced a takeover by GEC would have been a disaster for the concept of the company. Under Weinstock's control he doubted whether anything but the Inmos name would have lasted a year. Although the demise of GEC–Fairchild was never formally announced, it became increasingly evident, as the year wore on, that the joint venture was not to go ahead.

In the meantime the debate within the Cabinet continued

both about Inmos's factory location and whether it should be funded with another £25 million. On the location issue, the Inmos founders were gradually beginning to have second thoughts. In the Cabinet the Inmos preference for Bristol faced a formidable adversary in Nicholas Edwards who, as Welsh Secretary, had seen an NEB internal document which summarised the conclusions of the PA location study. Edwards thus knew that South Wales, only a few miles from Bristol, was considered a close second-best choice and he used the study's arguments, in the discussions he had with the Inmos management and the NEB, to support his own case. It appears that Edwards managed to persuade even Mrs Thatcher that a further investment in Inmos could be justified if it meant creating a substantial source of employment in job-hungry Wales. Although the three founders were convinced that they did not want the factory in the North of England and had subsequently agreed to hold out for Bristol, there was not total unanimity within the team. Petritz and Barron were keen on Bristol, but Schroeder had originally favoured Plymouth in Devon for a variety of excellent reasons.

First, as chief operating officer, Schroeder wanted the factory, which would be under his control, to be completely separate from Barron's microcomputer R&D operation; he saw the British plant as a high-volume manufacturing extension of the Colorado Springs facility more than the integrated 'mirror image' of the American operation that Petritz and Barron wanted. Secondly, like most Americans in the company, Schroeder had an absolute horror of trade unions. Both he and Petritz were worried about the strong tradition of trade unionism in Wales. Thirdly, Schroeder was a great believer in the importance of a company's image for its ultimate success. He had insisted, for example, on the Colorado Springs plan being an impressive building in attractive, residential, surroundings. He had visited Devon and liked the look of the place in contrast with South Wales which appeared dreary.

Plymouth had, incidentally, been put on the assisted area map by a Conservative review of industrial development policy after the PA study had been completed. The other two founders were still convinced, however, that an integrated facility still made the best sense for Inmos, not least because, apart from the technical synergy argument, a single building would both simplify management and save a considerable amount of investment on such costly overheads as telephone exchanges — a substantial saving for which it was by no means certain that any development grants would compensate.

As spring turned to summer, and the realisation that the funding and location decisions had become locked together gradually sank in, Petritz and Barron slowly warmed to the notion of a South Wales factory. The same reform which had created a development area in Devon had also pushed the assisted area boundary nearer to Bristol to include Newport, which apart from its greater proximity also was more pleasantly rural. Edwards, realising its attractions, was strongly selling Newport to the NEB. But the Inmos team, on balance, decided that it did not want to back down.

On the more fundamental issue of the second round of funding, the Cabinet seemed to be in deadlock. Twice Sir Keith had submitted the NEB's proposal and twice it had been rejected and Sir Keith asked to try again. Inmos had attempted to break the logjam in May with a high-powered sales pitch in the form of a presentation to interested politicians at the House of Commons of the firm's progress and potential; but this failed. In desperation Sir Arthur Knight had been trying to find alternative commercial sources of finance to try and safeguard the project in case the Government did not, finally, come through with the cash. His efforts had met with no success. Sir Keith himself had visited California's Silicon Valley at the end of May to learn more about the microchip business on its home ground. Inmos's competitors in the Valley could not have been expected to have been complimentary about the firm's

'As you can see, this is a terrible business to invest in.'

prospects, and the visit did not seem to have changed Sir Keith's thinking in any dramatic way.

As a last-ditch effort to swing the Cabinet towards a favourable decision, Sir Arthur decided to commission an independent inquiry into Inmos's prospects. He chose an NEB member, Sir George Jefferson, to lead the review. (Sir George was chairman of British Aerospace: he is now chairman and chief executive of British Telecom.) Sir George picked a team of experts from BAe with whom he flew out to Colorado Springs at the end of June. They were warmly welcomed. 'We were keen on the review. After all, we had somewhat "blindsided" (an American football term of obvious connotations) the new NEB board and thought it only fair they should take a good look at us,' recalled Petritz. The Jefferson team consisted of a group of specialists who were primarily looking at the company's management systems. In the mythology of Whitehall, Inmos was seen as just a bunch of 'boffins', amateurs, who were determined to squander the taxpayer's money, it must be remembered. In fact, Sir George's team was greatly impressed by the way the company was run and even said BAe could learn much from its methods. The Jefferson team was also impressed by the way Inmos had managed to stick to its expanded schedule in the United States. He was shown working samples of the 16k static and the development team could demonstrate considerable progress on the 64k dynamics. It all helped to show that Inmos had something real to offer.

Jefferson turned in a favourable report in July. It did, however, state that the company would probably need additional finance, on top of the second £25 million, to achieve its objectives. Sir George had actually warned Petritz during his visit to Colorado that the £8 million or £10 million that Inmos would gain in grants from locating in a development area would be very useful — an astute piece of advice which subsequent events were to prove fully justified. At the time Barron had thought the Jefferson study merely a cosmetic exercise designed to confirm the decision already made by the NEB and to provide it with a quotable document in case of subsequent disaster. In fact, however, it was to be Sir George's report that proved the critical factor in winning the Cabinet's approval for the second phase of investment.

Until July the basic message coming back from the Cabinet had been that it was not prepared to support the extra funding. The reason for its refusal had little or nothing to do with the location of the plant: it was just that the Inmos plans were fundamentally incompatible with Conservative philosophy. The two issues did get linked together, but more out of political expediency than a question of doctrine. While Sir George's team's favourable opinion of the company had finally swung the Cabinet round, Edwards's informed lobbying had also convinced it to make its approval conditional on the factory being built in Wales. The first the Inmos team heard of these developments was when they were called to an NEB meeting early in July. Ostensibly this was to discuss the Jefferson report, but it soon became clear to Petritz, Barron, Schroeder and Richard Hall, who was by then finance director, that its purpose was also to convey a Cabinet ultimatum.

Barron remembers this crucial meeting well:

> At the beginning of the meeting we were still saying that we wanted to go to Bristol and that anything else would compromise the operation of building a successful company. There was a presentation from Sir George, and we answered questions. The NEB's stance appeared neutral, the NEB participants just asked us for information. Then there was a big debate without us, we sat in an anteroom . . . when they had finished we were called back into the meeting, and were told they would not give us the £25 million unless we would go to South Wales. We went back into our anteroom and argued for two hours. Essentially at that time there were only three options: Bristol, South Wales and Plymouth. Paul was still very keen on Plymouth. Dick and I were firm on the factory being in Bristol. After a very long argument we went back to the NEB and said we still wanted to go to Bristol. We were politely told to go away and change our minds, because if we did not they would not support us. They didn't budge. They had their ploy and we had our ploy.
>
> We went out for about five minutes and then came back again. During the five minutes Paul mounted a furious argument in favour of Plymouth. Dick and I said Devon would be no more acceptable than Bristol. It would just have caused more problems if we went back and said 'we don't want South Wales but Plymouth will do'.

At this stage Petritz took a vote. Schroeder was the last to be polled and he finally agreed with the majority decision to pick South Wales. 'He took us right to the brink,' recalled Petritz.

Once the Inmos directors had finally capitulated over the Bristol location, the Government agreed within a few weeks to approve the second round of funding. The long, drawn-out wrangle had, however, been extremely painful and costly for the company. It created a nine-month delay in implementing its British production plans, with a consequent loss of output. This was valued at £46 million by opposition industry spokesman, John Silkin, in a Commons debate in July. The delay also reduced the firm's public credibility and damaged its already fragile relations with the press. And it certainly did little to boost internal morale. During the spring of 1980, for example, there had been a feeling at the American operation that if the firm had been forced to locate its British plant in a site that the Americans regarded as 'disastrous', then this would have sunk the whole company. There were thus many in Colorado Springs who felt that in such circumstances the firm should eschew the second £25 million from the Government and seek alternative sources of investment in the United States. Fortunately this vague disquiet never hardened into a positive action plan, but it was a close-run thing. Petritz looked back on the entire episode with regret:

> The whole issue could have been settled in March 1979, under a Labour Government, if we had agreed to locate in Cardiff, which was only 35 miles from Bristol.
> With hindsight the Inmos team must shoulder much of the blame for the delay and the damage it did. If we had chosen a development area site right from the start, our choice and the second £25 million would almost certainly have been approved straight away.

The hiatus in the firm's progress did, however, have one significant benefit. It enabled the management to make a thorough revision of its funding needs. By June 1980 it was becoming clear that the £50 million was not going to be enough. In the first year's operations Inmos had discovered the wonders of equipment leasing, but it needed the NEB to guarantee its lease commitments. When the Government finally approved the second tranche of money the Inmos board asked for, and got, an additional £35.3 million of lease guarantees. Petritz reckoned he was going back to the United States with £60 million rather than just the £25 million. But even that significant concession from the firm's backers was to prove troublesome. Inmos made one near-fatal error in failing to specify the exchange rate for the lease guarantees. The plan was based on two dollars to the pound, but what came back to haunt the board was the slide in the value of the pound. Inmos had used the second £25 million and the £35.5 million of lease guarantees to create debt in dollars with dollar repayments which it had to finance with pounds. But these were becoming worth less and less. When the Government had finally given the go-ahead, Petritz moved quickly to make peace with the firm's new-found ally in the Cabinet:

> The day I learned of the decision I called Sir Arthur and Nicholas Edwards with whom I had lunch. Despite the fact that he knew I had been opposed to locating in Wales originally, I soon established a good relationship with Edwards.

Richard Rogers, the architect of the Pompidou Centre in Paris, had already been commissioned to design a building. At the time Rogers was given the commission Inmos believed that it would be a building in Bristol. It had even acquired a site on top of a hill, just outside the city. In the end it kept the Rogers design but not the location. The rather splendid design intended for a West Country high point ended up in a Welsh field, with some of the original bits lost in the transition. It was still a very good design, however, regarded by many architectural historians as one of Rogers's finest.

Despite the urgent need to get going on the factory as soon as possible, there was another three-month delay before construction work could start. Having reluctantly agreed to a plant location close to Barron's Bristol technology centre, Schroeder then insisted that the plant would remain under his control. Barron says Schroeder started the whole process of conducting site studies afresh. This took a further two months. Before the second round of studies a site had been found near Cardiff. After the second round they eventually all agreed on one at Newport. The local council arranged the purchase at as dignified a rush as it could manage. There was finally a ceremonial ground-breaking in November. Even this was not a very auspicious start to the enterprise. It was a depressing day and pouring with rain. A television crew filmed in the middle of a muddy field but the item was never broadcast: the programme's editor did not think it sufficiently interesting. In the meantime, the Rogers design, an impressive suspended structure of the type which has since become rather fashionable, had been scaled down to suit the Newport site. The original plans allowed for 135,000 sq.ft. to house Barron's technology group as well as a manufacturing area. The Newport building only provided 85,000 sq.ft.

In the same month as the Newport ground-breaking, the composition of the Inmos board was radically altered by Sir Arthur. He did not want to have NEB members on the boards of NEB-sponsored or NEB-owned companies. A new system was introduced whereby Inmos reported progress every month to the NEB, but there were no NEB men on the board. Instead, the NEB appointed non-executive directors from outside industry and financial institutions. In November a new board was formally appointed. On to the board came Sir William Barlow. Until that summer he had been chairman of the Post Office and had then become chairman of the engineering group of Thorn–EMI. There were also three other new non-executive directors. The three founders, and the finance director, Richard Hall, were also on the new board.

Most important of all to Petritz was that he became chairman of Inmos, and was at the same time chief executive officer of the company. That change and the appointment of Sir William were both to prove highly significant events. On the very next day after the appointment of the four new non-executive directors, however, Sir Arthur himself resigned from the NEB. It appears that he had not been happy with the principle, or perhaps the details, of the merger between the NEB and the National Research Development Corporation which the Government intended to push through. Barron recalled Sir Arthur telling him and Petritz about his motives over dinner the night before his resignation:

> He put in the four non-executive directors the day before he resigned basically to ensure that we had some protection. His aim was to bring in some independent people to moderate the influence of the NEB and the Government.

Petritz also recalled the circumstances of the resignation, Sir Arthur not only disagreed about the merger; he was also ill and went off to see Sir Keith to ask for a few months' leave. 'I heard Sir Keith's reply to this request was "fine, don't bother to come back".' Prior to Petritz's appointment Inmos had not really had a proper, permanent, chairman. There was no formal chairman until then because Petritz wanted the job, the NEB would not give it to him and so Petritz had frustrated any attempt to appoint anyone else.

In practice the first chairman had been David Dunbar; when he left Dick Morris had taken over for one meeting; then Petritz was appointed. Petritz said later:

> So it was over two years from the company's formation that the NEB appointed me chairman and set up the new board. I had not minded not being chairman initially but as time went on it became more and more of an irritant. I had made it quite clear to Sir Arthur that if he liked what I was doing he ought to make me chairman and the other executives supported me in this. This

decision was well received by the company, most people preferred me to a complete outsider.

Barron was not totally convinced, however, whether, at least in one respect, Petritz was the ideal candidate. In particular, Barron suspected that the lack of a high-powered British chairman in early 1980 had severely hampered the firm's dealings with the Government:

> We suffered by not having a significant UK chairman. It was not until Sir Malcolm Wilcox took over nearly two years later that we had someone to represent the interests of Inmos at a significant level inside the UK establishment, somebody who was in a position to talk to Cabinet members with authority. I was the person who did that job but I never really had enough muscle to do it.

It was a curious weak spot in the firm's managerial line-up. Perhaps the reason is that there was continuing pressure on the NEB to prevent it allowing a Briton to be seen to be in charge. Both the Government and the NEB seemed to suffer from a national inferiority complex with respect to high technology. They both thought that Americans were better at it than the English, Scots, Welsh and Irish, and thus were reluctant to give anybody falling into any of the last four categories a chance a running a high-technology venture.

For Inmos 1981 started on an optimistic note. The traumas of the previous year seemed to be forgotten, and Petritz, in a new year interview looked forward to a 'year of transition from building a company to being an operating company'. In the same interview Petritz shrugged off the damage to the firm's strategy caused by the delay in establishing a British manufacturing facility, saying, 'it won't hurt us much'. Petritz was confident that Inmos would make an operating profit by the second half of 1982 and would achieve full profitability by the following year. He also stated categorically that Inmos would not ask the NEB for any more money and that, with the £50 million investment and £35 million of lease guarantees, the firm was well financed.

The new Inmos board got together for its first full meeting in January 1981 and there was plenty of progress to report. Inmos had made some management changes in July/August 1980. It had, for example, hired its first marketing vice-president, Doug Rankin, from Texas Instruments, who had soon got busy setting up a high-powered sales and marketing operation. The credentials of the five-man team Rankin put together read like a *Who's Who* of the semiconductor industry. Petritz was also able to report that the firm had made its first product deliveries, of the 16k sram, in December 1980. The new firm won $20,000–$30,000 of orders in that month, including one from Western Electric and another from IBM. It was understandably proud of these, as it was of the first shipment to the United Kingdom. Some chips went to Marconi at around the same time.

Inmos also saw what Petritz described as 'early signs of life' in

November 1980 in the samples of its 64k dynamic ram. The company's two initial products were thus both reasonably on schedule. 'So we went into the new year feeling pretty good,' remembered Petritz. The atmosphere at the first meeting of the new board, in Colorado Springs, was enthusiastic and charged with some optimism, at least as far as the Americans were concerned.

But even at this meeting, there were already signs of trouble brewing. Barron, who had been unhappy with the American management since the decision to build the Cheyenne Mountain plant, was opposed to what he regarded as the wild optimism represented by the latest plan put forward by his American colleagues. Based on the rapid progress to date, Petritz and Schroeder had estimated that the company could generate revenues of between £13 million and £14 million during 1981. Barron and his fellow British director, Richard Hall, said that it would take at least another year to build up production to this level.

The outside board members were bemused by this overt split between the executives, but nevertheless approved the plan which the Americans had presented. Thus, according to Barron, the confidence of the new non-executive directors was shaken right from the start. And, despite their initial enthusiasm, there was a growing feeling from then on amongst the outside board members that something was seriously wrong with the way the company was run.

By January the Colorado Springs building was advanced enough for Inmos to start moving equipment in and the Newport plant had at least progressed to being a muddy building site. The first silicon had been processed through the new line in Cheyenne Mountain in February/March, and the company was thus able to start forecasting its future operations. In April the company started an aggressive world-wide marketing drive. Apart from tackling the American market, the largest in the world, it appointed two firms to distribute its srams in Britain,

Hawke Cramer and Rapid Recall, which were chosen from a large number of high-technology distribution companies keen to share the profits generated by this already highly successful part. In Japan Inmos chose the Matsushita Electric Trading Company, a subsidiary of the world's largest consumer electronics maker, as its sales representative. Distributors and sales offices were also established a little later in every major European market. In April the newly appointed Minister for Information Technology, Kenneth Baker, visited Colorado Springs. Before his trip he remarked of Inmos merely that he was 'more pleased we have it than not'. On leaving, however, he said he was very impressed, and that the company was well up with the international front runners in the race to produce very large-scale integration chips.

However, just as the optimistic mood of the January meeting seemed to have been fully justified, the American operation ran into severe and widespread technical problems. With the static rams the initial yields had remained lower than 5 per cent, which meant that there were insufficient samples upon which to perform the tests and analyses required to identify and solve the problems. For the four new board members, none of whom had had any direct semiconductor experience, these difficulties came as a shock. Whilst it is true that the semiconductor business is too technically based not to have inevitable technical problems, the scale of these problems came as a severe blow to the outsiders. With the dram, for example, the designers were having trouble with the refresh circuits, so although the design looked fine it was not ready to put into production. In any case the firm did not have a specialised line on which to make the dram; Newport was still just a building site. So the Colorado Springs facility was trying to increase production and yield of the sram chips while at the same time pushing through batches of the dram to try to sort out the problem. In the semiconductor industry it is especially difficult to produce high volumes of different chips on the same fabrication line. Petritz admits:

We overestimated our ability to make two different products at the same time in the same facility. The dram and sram required different processing steps and in a new building with inexperienced staff, at the beginning of the learning curve, it was especially hard to mix and match the two types of chip.

Inmos also found itself in the middle of a severe chip recession in 1981. It did not, however, bother the company too much since its static ram was the only one on the market and it could sell as many as it could make. By June 1981 it was becoming increasingly clear that management changes needed to be made to cope with the conditions. During 1981, Barron became more and more vocal in his criticisms of Schroeder's management style:

> Paul is a brilliant person and most skilled at tasks requiring great attention to detail like designing chips; but running a company is more about getting the principles right. His style was to go off and do individual things to absolute perfection and lose sight of the strategy in the process.

Petritz had also gradually been coming around to this point of view, and had spent some time with Barron devising an alternative management structure for the company. They agreed during these discussions that the British and American operations should have two distant bosses and that Schroeder should not be one of them. It is ironic in the light of Barron's assessment of Schroeder's strengths that the role devised for him in the new regime was 'chief strategic officer', although the intention was quite sincerely to create a job in which Barron and Petritz felt he could be of real value to the firm.

The crunch came at a board meeting in June when the technical problems seemed at their worst. 'It was the only time the non-executive directors took positive action,' recalled Barron, 'they were tough in their criticisms of the company's progress and demanded each of us not only to account for our shortcomings but also to suggest what needed to be done.' The board was presented with the Barron/Petritz reorganisation plan and seized upon it eagerly. Schroeder was somewhat surprised by the plot to depose him but reluctantly agreed to take up the new job. So John Heightley was made president of Inmos Corporation, and in effect became chief operating officer. Barron was made managing director of Inmos Ltd., which was a largely self-sufficient operation at that time, and he also took control of Newport. Schroeder's job of chief operating officer was not formally filled after he had been persuaded to step down.

At the end of June 1981, three British journalists were visiting Colorado Springs on the day Petritz had what he described as 'discussions' with Schroeder on the reorganisation. The pressmen did not notice the upheaval and instead picked up on a remark Petritz made about Inmos eventually having a Japanese operation as an essential prerequisite to getting into that very important market. Although this was clearly a long-term plan, the journalists, hard-pressed for a dramatic story, wrote as if Inmos were going to break ground on the Japanese plant the very next week, and missed the far more important story of the resignation of one of the three founders. For, although Schroeder had initially accepted his suggested change of role, on later reflection he had decided that the job was not what he wanted and that the board's decision amounted to constructive dismissal. The settlement of this dispute took nearly a year, but Schroeder ceased being active in the company in September, and resigned as a director in the spring of the following year. In the end, he retained his founder's shareholding, to which he had an absolute right, and was given over two years' salary, some $240,000, as compensation for loss of office.

Despite the circumstances of his departure, Petritz felt that Schroeder has been very important at Inmos in getting the company started. His contribution to Mostek had, incidentally, also helped make Petritz's Mostek shares worth a lot of money. Schroeder, like many brilliant engineers, had felt that at a certain stage in his career he wanted to move into general management. Petritz had brought him into Inmos on that basis and had made that clear to the NEB. With hindsight, however, Petritz felt that the NEB never really appreciated Schroeder's new role; they had thought that he had been personally designing all Inmos's drams. Schroeder was, after all, regarded as the world's best dynamic memory designer, he had revolutionised the business with the Mostek 4k and 16k devices, and Petritz had thought that he would be the right person to put the Inmos design group together, but that he should not actually do the designing himself. 'He did exactly what we had expected,' remembered Petritz, but as a day-to-day manager, John Heightley seemed better for the job.

It was not just the NEB, but the whole outside world, that thought that Schroeder was responsible for all of Inmos's designs. He was under considerable pressure. One of Petritz's visions for Inmos had been to combine the design and process development skills of institutions like Bell Laboratories with the manufacturing, marketing and financial acumen of Texas Instruments. According to Petritz, Schroeder and Heightley built up the company's strengths in the former area. 'The first semiconductor start-up I was involved with, Mostek, did not achieve the overall quality of Inmos's R&D outfit,' argued Petritz:

> This is because it spun off directly from TI. I believe that the second time round I have managed to help to build a far better company. It is not only a multinational outfit but also a multifaceted firm in terms of the management personalities, unlike some US chipmakers which are dominated by a single boss.

After Heightley took over as president, Inmos began steadily to overcome its problems and, in the opinion of many of his colleagues, he proved to be a good manager. The board had been concerned that since Heightley's background was similar to Schroeder's — they had both come out of Bell Labs rather than a business school — there was no reason to believe he would do any beter. Petritz had, however, got to know Heightley very well over almost three years of working together, so he was convinced that he had the qualities to do the job well. At the time, however, it was a very big step for Heightley to move from design manager to president.

During that tumultuous summer Inmos had moved all its production into the Cheyenne Mountain plant and was only using the Harrison Park temporary plant as a testing area. By the end of the year the company had shipped $4 million worth of 16k statics, not a trivial number, but way below the turnover predicted by the business plan about which Barron and Hall had been so sceptical. (In fact, Barron's initial plan foresaw a £30 million turnover for 1981, based mostly on drams, but this had long since been abandoned in the light of the early selection of the sram as first priority and the delays of the previous year.) The 1981/2 recession in the chip business could not be blamed for the company running behind schedule; its problems were concerned far more with supply than with demand. Inmos could sell all it could make but just could not make enough product.

To put Inmos's production problems in perspective, Intel had announced its own 16k static a year ahead of the IMS1400, and had been talking to the market about its own part but had never delivered. In 1981 Inmos fully expected Intel to become a competitor along with the Japanese, but neither immediately materialised and the company had a temporary monopoly. Inmos had, however, been very aggressive in its use of technology; it was committed to the use of wafer-steppers and dry (plasma) etching for a lot. of the process steps, both relatively new and untried techniques. Inmos was also the first company to use redundancy in a commercial chip. This latter feature helped increase yield in the long run but it took a while to get it working.

Such was the demand for its statics, however, that Inmos could sell them at over $100 each. One of the reasons for the company's ambitious marketing plan was that it had expected Intel to prepare the market, and was not aware early enough that Intel had failed to deliver. This did not affect Inmos's actual sales but it made its target shortfall that much greater, which did not impress the new board. Despite the initial problems created by its choice of untried process technologies, Petritz is convinced that the strategy was correct: 'I am sure we would not be selling so many statics now (they still formed the bulk of Inmos's sales in 1985) if we had taken a more cautious short-term view.' The problems with the static rams had nevertheless shaken yet further the board's confidence in the Inmos management's ability to plan. Although those board members without a background in the industry had been horrified by the firm's apparently poor performance, it is by no means unusual for semiconductor start-ups to do only around $4 million worth of business in their first year of production.

At the end of 1981 the new Inmos team made its next plan, which it thought was fairly modest at the time, to sell between $25 million and $30 million worth of statics in the coming year. As it turned out, 1982 was still a recession year, yet despite the general slump the company managed to achieve the lower end of its sales target. Petritz recalled:

> We did not sell as many parts as we had hoped but the static was very popular with the military and we made a lot of sales at military premium prices. The board congratulated us in growing sales from $4 million to $25 million, but it really wasn't an exceptional achievement for a semiconductor start-up.

The company's technologists had also debugged the 64k dram design by early 1982, so an attempt was made to put it into production at Colorado Springs. The delays in getting the British facility had, however, put the dram well behind schedule from a production point of view. Inmos had tried to run the dram through the Colorado Springs facility from the summer of 1981 and even though dram batches were kept at a fairly low level, the manufacturing operation still found considerable difficulty in producing the two products in the same plant. 'We ran a few thousand dram wafers a month for a five to six week period to try and debug the process and found it was just too much for us to handle,' remembered Petritz with regret. By the beginning of 1982, Intel had publicly announced that it was withdrawing from the 16k sram business; it just could not match the specifications of the Inmos devices, so the only competition came from the Japanese. 'We had a nice, profitable, static ram business and, if we had not have been building Newport, Inmos would have been profitable in 1982,' said Petritz in defence of one of his January 1981 predictions.

A major contributor to the operational profitability of Inmos during 1982 was the introduction, in August 1981, of its second family of static rams. Unlike the IMS1400, these parts were organised so that 4 bits of information could be read and written into the chip at the same time. The IMS1420 parts (there were three versions wth slightly different speeds and features) were among the first chips to adopt this 4 bit-wide architecture which was later to become extremely popular with equipment designers. The IMS1420 chips consequently managed to command a substantial price premium over conventional 16k srams.

By the end of 1981 about fifty engineers and managers had been recruited, mostly in the United Kingdom, to run the Newport plant and were working in Colorado Springs to learn the way Inmos made chips. In the meantime, however, the pound had begun its steady decline against the dollar and the Inmos management realised that it did not have enough money to bring Newport up to full production. The company was forced to buy all of its production equipment in the United States and pay for it, or for the leases, in ever more costly US dollars.

At first, srams were made at Newport in order to get the wrinkles out of its newly established manufacturing system, at a rate of only 500 wafers per month (barely above prototype quantities), with a single shift of workers on a single line. Petritz and Barron told the NEB, whose chairman was Sir Freddie Wood by then, that the company could not afford to build up production to full volume on that single line, let alone set up the planned second line, without an extra injection of funds. The management therefore asked for another £15 million that summer and the NEB, now merged with the National Research Development Corporation to form the British Technology Group, and with totally new management, decided that it wanted yet another consultant's report on the state of the company. Integrated Circuit Engineering of Phoenix, Arizona, was brought in and embarked on another 'Is Inmos to succeed?' study. Glenn Madland, a consultant at ICE, undertook the study and gave the firm yet another clean bill of health.

On its own initiative the company had also hired Hill Samuel around then to try to find it some other sources of finance. Inmos did not want to ask the British Government for more finance if it could possible avoid doing so. But Hill Samuel's advice to the board was that it could not raise the money either from institutions or private investors. It had proved impossible to convince any potential investors that the extra £15 million was needed simply to meet exchange-rate losses. Rumours that the company was in deep trouble were widespread and thus there was no viable alternative to asking the Government for the money. The performance of the American end of the company was broadly in line with the plan the NEB had approved. Petritz therefore hoped there would be no problem in persuading the Government to come up with the money. The Inmos board agreed to ask for the additional £15 million in

August 1982. In September the favourable Madland report came in and the Inmos team had many meetings with the NEB and the Treasury that autumn.

The Government had three options: it could allow Inmos to raise money through normal commercial channels in increasing its borrowing limit for which the state was ultimately responsible: it could put a further £15 million in equity; or it could abandon the whole project. By January 1983, the NEB (now part of the BTG) and the Government had finally decided to invest the extra £15 million. The firm was told, however, that this was 'absolutely the last bit of cash it would get'.

Yet again the negotiations had been tortuous. The NEB had wanted to pay only £3.00 a share for its further injection of equity. This would have halved the founders' and employees' interest in the firm and was thus strongly resisted by the Inmos management. Instead, they wanted the NEB to make its investment at the original negotiable price for preference shares of £20.00 or more. At one stage in the talks, Petritz walked out and flew back to the United States in disgust at the NEB's intransigence. Eventually, however, a compromise had been hammered out whereby the NEB's new shareholding would be valued according to a formula based on the company's future performance. The eventual value placed on the fresh shareholding was £17.00, far nearer the initial offer price that anyone at the NEB suspected it would be at the time.

There were also strings attached to the deal. The main concession Inmos had to make was the appointment of Sir Malcolm Wilcox as chairman. It was clear that the NEB, having put in the extra money, finally had decided that it wanted the company to be seen to be run by a Briton, and to have a chairman who could prepare it for privatisation. So, Petritz lost the chairmanship he had so recently gained — the job he had made clear from the outset that he really wanted. But he gave in gracefully and did not seriously try and resist his demotion.

Later he rationalised the position by pointing our that if the extra money was to be raised in Britain then the price that would have to be paid was the appointment of a British chairman. Petritz may have had notions about going to the American stockmarket to find the money, but the ownership of the company was firmly in British hands and both the British owners and the British employees had other ideas about the future financing of the company.

It might seem strange that Petritz should give way without an acrimonious public fight. Schroeder had, after all, resigned when he had been moved sideways into a specially created post, and in Petritz's case it was an unambiguous demotion. Further, the new part-time head of the firm was to be a London-based banker, the primary loyalty of whom would never be to the young company in Colorado Springs. The explanation is that Petritz and the rest of the American team demanded and got a large reward for their agreement to the appointment of Sir Malcolm. On top of the £15 million they secured complete control of the day-to-day operations of the company in the United Kingdom, with the exception of the Bristol design centre.

For some time the firm's non-executive directors had been under pressure from the American team to appoint a new boss at Newport and, in January, Heightley was the man they chose. Incidentally, they also appointed him to the company's main board. In July 1981, when Schroeder effectively left the company, control of the Newport wafer fabrication plant had crossed the Atlantic and Barron, as British managing director, had taken over. One of his early actions was to dismiss the manager at Newport, Rex Mears, who had been appointed by Paul Schroeder.

Mears had seemed ideal for the task, having gained experience in the British semiconductor industry as a senior manager and as a workers' representative (trade-union shop steward) earlier in his career. Who better to deal with the union sensitivities of the Welsh work-force? Unfortunately, Mears's political inclinations proved not to be a great asset to the firm. 'He spent more time on company politics than on getting the plant running,' said Heightley; 'he seemed to think Newport was to be a silicon foundry for the whole of UK industry rather than a company factory.'

Barron's choice turned out to be unacceptable to the American chip experts. Unable to find a plant manager of adequate calibre in the United Kingdom, Mike Wright, the personnel specialist and long-time associate of Barron, was assigned the job on a temporary basis. Wright, the American team felt, was a fine manager but lacked the detailed skills and, above all, experience to set up a semiconductor plant. After having wrested control of Newport away from the United States, Barron was naturally reluctant to allow an American to take charge. Yet, unfortunately, the vast majority of experienced chip-factory managers were, and still are, to be found in the United States. Heightley conceded that Barron's patriotism 'may have blinded him to the shortcomings of his own appointee', but he was nevertheless determined to get Newport run by a man with the necessary specialised skills and appropriate background.

There was a second bone of contention, namely, which product Newport should be allowed to make. The choice was between the 16k static ram or the 64k dynamic ram. The original policy of the company had been to transfer products from Colorado Springs to Newport for volume production. The British team wanted to follow this policy and manufacture the 16k static ram at Newport. The American team wanted to retain the 16k static in Cheyenne Mountain and transfer the 64k dynamic ram. But this latter part still had major manufacturing problems. The technical arguments raged back and fourth, whilst the real issues were not really discussed, recalled Barron in retrospect.

The 16k static was a highly profitable part with a secure

market; the 64k part was unproven, was unlikely to be very profitable and was competing in uncertain markets against the major Japanese and American suppliers. The commercial climate had changed radically since the first business plan had been written in 1979, when the 64k dynamic ram had been seen as the key entry product. Now, if the United States concentrated on the static ram it would be a highly profitable operation and the opportunity to break away as an independent company would be correspondingly larger. Again the United States won the argument and the United Kingdom was given the task of making the 64k dynamic ram into a part that could be realistically mass-produced. The consequences of this decision were not to become apparent until the collapse of the semiconductor market in 1985.

Determined or not, Heightley and Petritz would not have stood a chance of gaining control of the British plant if it had been performing efficiently. But the arrival of a crop of production problems — they tend to plague any new semiconductor facility and have a habit of coming at just the wrong time — made it very difficult for Barron to argue that the existing arrangements had been working well. The non-executive directors seem to have been in a state of panic by this time. It would have been quite feasible for them to have insisted that someone come over from the United States to work under Barron.

Instead, the board not only took away the British plant from him but also the responsibility for marketing activities. In future these operations were to report directly to Colorado Springs. Heightley became the chief of all of Inmos's operations in the United States and the United Kingdom. He was president in the United States already; now his presidential power embraced most of Inmos's activities in Britain. Petritz might not have been chairman any more, but he probably had more day-to-day power over the activities of the company than ever before. When Heightley took over, his first action was to dispatch another American, Ralph Bohannon, to take charge of the whole Newport operation.

The British management was aghast at the reorganisation of the company and prepared to resign *en masse*. For a second time Barron did resign, arguing again that the company was not being run in the best interests of its major shareholder, the NEB now repackaged as the BTG. The BTG, however, did not see things quite like this. Instead it threatened to put the company into liquidation if the resignation was not withdrawn. The threat was sufficient to keep Barron in line and presumably to get him to defuse the explosive atmosphere that was building up around the other British staff. He later said that he feared that the NEB would indeed go through with the action and, if it had been put into practice, all of the Inmos staff would have been thrown out of a job with no compensation, as the company had no funds for redundancy payments.

Barron was thus neatly boxed in. Most of the control of the company was stripped away from him but if he refused to go along with the plan then the company's main backer seemed prepared to close down the whole enterprise. The British press got wind of this major shift in the firm's geographical power centre, probably through a leak made by a civil servant, but the newspaper accounts of the changes, as had become usual in relation to Inmos, were not quite right. A *Sunday Times* article on 16 January 1983 claimed that Inmos had 'decided to concentrate its most profitable production in America' and that the decision had been made without the knowledge of the Government or the BTG. 'The American operation has become dominant,' the paper claimed. Inmos, it said, was proposing to centre the manufacture of the one profitable part it had at the time, the 16k static, in the United States. It went on to claim that in place of the proven and profitable 16k static, Newport would get the chancy 64k dynamic ram, which had yet to prove itself and was up against intense international competition. The Sunday Times said that its revelations would cause a major row.

And indeed they did, even if some of the information was incorrect. The BTG and the Government had known what was happening. Otherwise the story was 'spot on' and the product moves were to alter radically the shape of the company for many years to come. It had been assumed that, because Inmos now had a British chairman, power was in British hands. In reality the British executives now had less power than at any time since the formation of the firm. A few days later Kenneth Baker, the Information Technology Minister denied the main substantive points of the *Sunday Times* story. He did not, though, see fit to point out that the power structure of the company had just altered dramatically.

9   The Challenge of the Transputer

Despite all the corporate and political turmoil, it must be remembered that the company had been growing all the time. Put crudely, by 1983 Inmos was something worth fighting over. Apart from the two facilities at Cheyenne Mountain and Newport, there was the British Design Centre. This had been painstakingly built up during 1980 and thereafter emerged as one of the company's most important assets, although it has to be said that many of the Americans regarded it as something of a joke for a long time.

In some ways, setting up a design team in the United Kingdom capable of turning out products at the leading edge of semiconductor technology was even more difficult than setting up an efficient and profitable semiconductor manufacturing facility in the United States. Attracting staff of the right calibre was a very big problem. 'It was really quite impracticable to attract the right people to work in the UK,' recalled Barron; 'bright engineers were reluctant to move to what they saw as a technology backwater and, in any case, we could not have afforded them.' Technologists in the United States felt, with considerable justification, that they were working where the technical action was, and that they would lose their edge if they went to work in Bristol.

Even if they could have been dissuaded from this view, it would have cost the company around £90,000 a year, according to Barron's calculations, for the full expatriate package each would have demanded. This was just for fairly standard engineers; those with substantial track records or managerial experience would have been even more costly. Apart from the sheer expense involved in recruiting from the

United States, It would have created massive personnel problems to have people on American pay scales working alongside those hired in Britain for a relative pittance. But many amongst the British press had expected Inmos to bring back high-flying technologists to Britain. Several British papers ran stories on the 'reverse brain drain', and all were disillusioned when nothing happened. This failure to recruit in the United States illustrates two of the firm's recurring problems at this time: its lack of credibility with the British press and the massive disparity between the amount paid to its employees on either side of the Atlantic. The problem of salary differentials has continued to deteriorate. 'When we started the firm, the ratio of US salaries to those in the UK was about two to one,' said Barron; 'now it is nearer three to one'. These were relatively minor problems for the British management, however, since its toughest challenge was neither improving its public image nor recruitment but rather the consolidation of its existing team.

One result of the troubles of 1980 had been that Barron had been able to spare very little time actually to manage the company. This was especially damaging since, although Barron had hired a set of individuals with considerable imagination and originality, many of the brighter designers had adopted quite contradictory views about what needed to be done, and what form Inmos's first microcomputer should take. All at Inmos's technology centre agreed that the initial microcomputer offering should be a total break with the traditions of the past. For too long British computer experts had been forced to use the designs originating from the United States, and, frustrated by their own inability to manufacture a satisfactory alternative, British experts, along with their colleagues in Europe, had become the sharpest and most vociferous critics of existing trends in microprocessor development.

The microprocessor, the heart of a digital computer on a single cheap chip of silicon, had been invented almost by accident by a Silicon Valley firm, Intel, in 1971. In response to a request from a Japanese maker of pocket calculators, Intel had designed a chip, the 4004, which could be programmed to perform a wide variety of calculator functions. In this context the chip's 'programmability' consisted of its ability to read, and act upon, a set of instructions that were stored in a separate chip memory (not like those made by Inmos but more primitive, called a read only memory, or rom). The 4004 and the chips that were developed from it were thus like the largest computers, very flexible in their operation because they were adaptable to the execution of a wide range of tasks by the provision of different stored programs. The problem was, from the point of view of the Bristol experts, that the various families of processor chips which had been evolved from Intel's pioneering part all shared its original limitations.

The 4004 had been designed to perform simple arithmetic functions in an efficient manner; the kind of instructions it could understand were therefore made up of such simple types as 'add', 'subtract', 'store' and 'multiply'. Later chips simply extended the instruction range to include the kind of functions found in the large computers of the 1960s: 'branching' instructions to enable the program to choose alternative options according to the values of the variables it was dealing with, and 'interrupt' instructions to allow the processor temporarily to stop calculating while a problem generated by another chip in the system was sorted out. Although such chips increased vastly in sophistication during the 1970s, such development was based on the original structure (architecture) of the original devices. More and more instructions were introduced to cope with the need for microprocessors to handle textual (alphanumeric) information as well as numbers, and the most advanced products could cope with the manipulation of pictures in the form of patterns of dots (pixels).

Microprocessors also became faster at processing instructions and dealt with ever larger chunks of information in a given time period. The 4004, for example, could only deal with numbers between 0 and 15, represented by four digital bits (larger numbers could be handled by combining a series of operations). By 1978 the latest processor chips could cope with numbers between 0 and 65536, made up of 16 bits. Since 8 bits are effectively needed to encode a single alphanumeric character, 16-bit chips, like the Intel 8086 and Motorola 68000, were far better than their predecessors at not only doing fast arithmetic but also manipulating patterns of words and pictures. Chips had also incorporated more and more of the extra functions, such as the ability to store data and accept it as input from, for example, a keyboard, or to send it out to a screen. Such more highly integrated chips were known as microcomputers rather than microprocessors.

But the purists at Inmos still thought processor architecture had taken a wrong turning when it started slavishly to copy the features of pocket calculators and early large computers. For Barron, and for the others in the team he had recruited, the full potential of the mos silicon chip would not be fully exploited without devising a more appropriate architecture. The main difficulty was that the young British 'whizz-kids' in Bristol had totally failed to agree on what the ideal architecture should look like. While Barron should have been acting as referee, and ultimate arbiter, in the intellectual discussions taking place at Bristol, he had, instead, been doing his best to ensure the company's future by arguing with the politicians. By the summer of 1980, Inmos's microcomputer strategy was in a shambles. Barron recalled:

All of our people had different ideas and were failing to shake down together because there was nobody there to give them a strong lead. I was too busy off dealing with the politics to provide enough positive input. The delay over our funding not only held up the setting up of production in the UK but also seriously hampered the development of our microprocessor products.

Two of the main protagonists in Bristol were David May and Robert Milne. May had been recruited from Warwick where he had been a disciple of Tony Hoare, an academic guru who, when he had worked with Barron before, had chosen a professorial post at Belfast University rather than joining Computer Technology, Barron's first firm. Milne had been hired from Scicon, a large London-based firm specialising in the production of complex computer programs. Before then, he had worked with Chris Stratchey, a leading computing expert, at the Programming Research Group of Oxford University. In the absence of Barron, both May and Milne had taken up inflexible positions over their choice of the most desirable architecture for Inmos's 'Transputer' chip.

Milne favoured a design specifically tailored to work with a particular high-level programming language, 'Ada', which had been developed at the request of the United States' Department of Defense. The Department of Defense had been worried about the vast diversity of programming languages used by its large number of equipment contractors. Ada was designed, therefore, to be a general-purpose language in which instructions could be written to do anything from guiding nuclear missiles to sorting out the payroll for the Oakland Navy base. High-level languages had been developed to cut the cost of producing the vast amount of software needed to run the ever-growing number of computer-based applications. Instead of programming a chip, or a large computer, with a set of elementary binary instructions which it could immediately 'understand', a separate program, called a 'compiler', was devised which was used to translate commands written in an approximation to English (or another ordinary natural language) into the patterns of noughts and ones the computer chips could deal with.

Unfortunately, various specialist languages had grown up that were all tailored to the solution of different kinds of problems: Fortran and Algol for mathematical applications, for example, Cobol for commercial systems and Pascal for handling systems which needed an instant response from the control computer (so-called 'real time' systems). Not only were each of these languages fundamentally different from each other; often two versions of the 'same' language produced at different times or by rival manufacturers would not be mutually compatible. The Department of Defense's Ada initiative was thus designed to resolve the increasing problem of computer Babel by producing a single, all-purpose, standard language.

Although Ada faced problems right from the start, since so much time and effort had been put into writing programs in existing languages and training programmers in their use, there were many who felt that the massive influence, and huge purchasing power, of the United States' military would be sufficient to establish Ada as a new world-wide standard. This view was especially prevalent within the many companies that made considerable profits from supplying complex military software. These software houses saw the advent of Ada as a unique opportunity for foreign firms to break into the lucrative American defence market. Milne favoured this approach for the Transputer: that it should be the first chip in the world specifically tailored to run Ada.

This approach was anathema to Tony Hoare, even though Ada incorporated some of his own ideas, and to his disciples at Inmos. For Hoare, the trend in high-level language development, towards ever more complex features to cope with ever-expanding application areas, was a basic mistake. As languages became increasingly complicated it became more and more difficult to work out whether the translations they produced were correct. This criticism, according to Hoare, was especially relevant to real time systems, and particularly worrying in connection with such systems as these used by the military. Languages like Ada, Hoare argued, were so complex that no one would ever know if a missile, or early warning system, had been correctly programmed, and the consequences of such a failure would be truly disastrous. Hoare was, in computing terms, a fundamentalist, and May and Barron had been raised in the same creed. What they all wanted was a new simplicity in computers, in their structure and in the languages used to program them. In this context simplicity need not be the enemy of performance. Indeed, Barron and May thought a simply-structured chip might be capable of far faster operation than the existing ranges of complex devices. By increasing the elegance of architectures and languages, the full potential of mos chips — their ability to perform lots of elementary operations at speeds approaching that of light — could be fully harnessed.

The Milne/May debate was not to be resolved for some time. Some essential decisions had, however, been taken at a very early stage and they were no less revolutionary in their implications than the choice of instruction format and programming approach. Since 1977 Barron had been arguing that the microcomputer of the future would inevitably incorporate a certain amount of random access memory. Many such devices had already been launched by 1980, but the memory had always been added almost as an afterthought. In Barron's view, processing and memory (used to store instructions and the data that were being manipulated) were so closely associated as to become eventually indistinguishable. The transputer was therefore designed from scratch to combine memory and processing capability. If every microcomputer could have intimate access to its own data, argued Barron, then it would be much easier to design systems that put together a multiplicity of microprocessors to tackle really tricky problems like understanding human speech. Here was another fundamental point of computing philosophy: rather than trying constantly to improve the speed and power of an individual processor, Barron was convinced that the way ahead lay in harnessing the power of lots of small processors together to provide the most cost effective way of building ever more capable computers.

Hence one arrives at the third major revolutionary aspect of the Transputer: the means by which it communicated with other devices. Conventional processors communicate with other chips, and with the input and output devices of the system of which they are a part, via a 'bus'. This consists of a set of wires, one for each bit that the chip is capable of handling simultaneously, which links all the devices together. If one chip needs to send data to another, it first has to establish whether the bus is free, then transmit the data preceded by a signal representing the 'address' of the intended recipient, and it then has to send another signal to check if the data have been received correctly. Although the bus is simple in physical form and concept, its use in practice is quite complicated even if only a few parts are hooked up to it. If a system consists of a large number of chips, managing the data traffic on the bus gets tricky and special chips, called 'bus drivers', have to be used to regulate the data flow.

For Barron's vision of a powerful computing engine made up of multiplicity of individual processors all working at the same time (concurrently), the bus concept is unworkable since the chips would spend more time managing internal communications than actually processing data. The alternative approach was to give each processor a fixed number of communication circuits, which it could manage for itself, and allow each circuit to be linked directly to one other similar part. This point-to-point communications approach was a great leap into the unknown since buses had been around for long enough for every designer to have become familiar with their use and for a variety of different standards to have emerged and found almost universal acceptance. So, while it had been decided early on to incorporate a large, fast memory on the transputer chip and adopt a radical new method of communications, the detailed structure of the transputer had still not been chosen by as late as the beginning of 1981.

In the end, Barron grew tired of waiting for a consensus to

emerge from his team and decided to enforce his own preference. Along with May, Barron had decided that the transputer should be what others now describe as a 'reduced instruction set computer' (risc). Instead of the hundreds of different types of instructions recognised by the most sophisticated conventional processor chips, the Transputer would only use a small number. With its reduced instruction set, on chip memory and direct communications, the transputer was seen as an ideal device to control for example, the next generation of home appliances, and factory automation equipment. The same virtues that suited it for these tasks would also make it easier to link several transputers together to tackle more general-purpose computing applications. This is not to say that the transputer's risc architecture would prevent it from providing a high level of processing performance. On the contrary, the risc theory suggests that, since out of any instruction set only 10 per cent of the instructions are used in 90 per cent of cases, the performance penalty imposed by having to construct the more esoteric instructions out of the simple ones is more than outweighed by the gain in throughput obtained by making sure that the most common ones are executed in the most efficient fashion.

May was given the job of designing the risc transputer in the spring of 1981. But Barron tried once again to involve Milne in the project, even though his architectural idea had been firmly rejected. Milne was thus asked to design a programming language which would complement May's risc hardware. But still the team could not reach agreement. Milne wanted to write a better version of Ada, which just did not fit in with the essential simplicity of the transputer architecture.

After six months' wrangling, Barron again had to put his foot down. The language was to be as simple and elegant as the transputer structure itself. Barron, Hoare and May went off to a hotel for a week-long brainstorming session and returned with the specification for the new language. Milne's final contribution, before resigning and going to work for British Telecom, was to dream up a name for the language. William of Occam was an early English philosopher who had proposed that philosophy should 'not multiply entities without necessity'. Known as 'Occam's razor', this principle had been adopted by later, and greater, British thinkers such as Bertrand Russell. It also seemed to epitomise the Inmos approach to computing, so the name 'occam' won the naming competition organised by Barron outright. It was an unfortunate irony that Barron had offered a case of champagne as the prize, for Milne was a teetotaller and was thus unable to enjoy it.

Occam was just as revolutionary as any other aspect of the transputer. It was intended not just as a programming language but also as a means of describing the structure of a computing system. It bucked the trend in the evolution of computer languages towards ever greater sophistication and complexity. It was not oriented towards specific applications, but allowed programmers to write compilers for higher-level languages that were. And above all it was simple, being defined in terms of a few primitive constructs from which more complex structures could be built. By September 1981, when the occam specification was published, most of the ingredients of the transputer had finally been sorted out, but the job was far from over. The agonisingly difficult and risky business of actually transforming a bunch of radical ideas into a working and saleable piece of silicon required two further, and vital, components: a design system and a manufacturing process.

By the 1980s, the procedures for designing silicon chips had to some extent been automated. The semiconductor industry had been one of the first to exploit its own products in the form of computer systems to aid the chip designer in laying out the complex patterns of the various layers of an integrated circuit. Other systems were also used to simulate the performance of the finished article before it was actually made and to take over the tedious task of preparing the test routines and the actual photographic masks used during manufacture. A healthy industry had grown up supplying such specialised design tools, and at Colorado Springs, for example, the Inmos team had purchased all the necessary equipment from Silicon Valley suppliers. The staff at Bristol had, however, rejected such an option right from the start. Deciding that existing equipment was not powerful enough for the task of designing the complex random logic circuits needed to make a transputer. Inmos had set up a team of five people in the spring of 1980 to build a set of ideal chip design tools from scratch. By the time the ultimate form of the transputer had been finalised it was still by no means certain whether this home-grown design system would eventually work. It was not until 1983 that the Inmos computer aided design system, which had been codenamed 'Fat Freddy' after an American hippie cartoon character, was finally to prove itself.

The second missing ingredient was a manufacturing process. It had originally been intended that the transputer should be designed to use the same process as the 64k dynamic ram. But this approach had been vetoed by Paul Schroeder, who had argued that the risks involved were too high because the operation of the processor might interfere with the very delicate mechanism of the on-chip dynamic ram. In the jargon used by chip designers, this problem, when it does occur, is known as 'noise'. The decision to abandon dram technology in favour of the theoretically more stable sram route put a major delay into the transputer programme. This was because the 16k static ram process would not support the level of complexity required for the transputer, and so the transputer design was forced to wait for the development of the next generation 64k static ram technology.

The transputer designers reviewed the technology options and came to the conclusion that the best available technology for both the transputer and the next generation memory products was cmos — complementary metal-oxide semi-conductors — the coming thing at the time. Its intrinsic, low-power requirements and other advantages made it ideal for making most chips, and it was gradually being realised that cmos would also be needed to make any very complex chip. With so many functions packed into a tiny area, power dissipation was becoming a critical variable. Even with the mainstream nmos technology, which was much less power-hungry than bipolar, and which it had largely displaced for digital applications, it was becoming harder to increase chip density without running into problems with the amount of heat generated. Opinions differed, however, about how much growth potential could be extracted, by design ingenuity, from the inherently much simpler nmos process. Inmos's memories had all been made in nmos, and the Colorado Springs group saw no need to develop cmos technology. They argued back and forth across the Atlantic on the subject until 1982 when Colorado Springs needed to develop a process for its next generation memory products and finally came to appreciate the advantages of cmos.

Even then the transputer was not out of the woods. Its future was dependent on the United States developing a process and manufacturing the prototypes. The development of the cmos process was slow. In consequence, a queue of new products built up for prototyping in Colorado Springs. This queue was made up of a range of 64k static rams, a range of 64k dynamic rams and the transputer tagging along behind. Just as in 1982 Colorado Springs had found it difficult to start up the manufacture of the 64k dynamic ram while manufacturing the 16k statics in volume, so the same problems were experienced in 1983 and 1984 as the new generation products came on to the production-line.

As a result the British designers were only to receive three batches of working silicon prototypes of the transputer during 1983 and 1984. It made the target Barron had announced for transputer samples look rather foolish. In the event, midnight on 31 December 1984 went by without a transputer to be seen.

Although the public reaction to the transputer had been enthusiastic, even by 1985 it was too early to tell whether the transputer was a potential moneyspinner or just a brilliant concept that was so radical in every aspect to be way ahead of its time.

The reactions of Inmos's American staff to the transputer saga had been somewhat bemused. Most Americans, both within the company and outside it, had been deeply impressed by the chip's intellectual concepts; Barron had addressed a huge audience at a Silicon Valley electronics exhibition in the autumn of 1983 and had been delighted with the warmth of the response. One American chip-maker had offered to make the transputer under licence, an offer Barron had refused until it could be negotiated on the more favourable terms made possible by having actual chips to sell. But the American Inmos employees could not understand the desperate need of those in Bristol to challenge every single convention of microcomputer design. In particular, it was hard for those in Colorado Springs to understand why the British team had decided to build its own design tools. 'For a start-up company trying to get products out very quickly, that did not look like a very good idea,' commented Heightley. The seemingly endless wrangles over the precise structure of the transputer chip were also incomprehensible to the Americans, as was the Bristol team's insistence on the next generation process for their brainchild.

These differing perceptions illustrate the great contrast between Inmos's staff on either side of the Atlantic. Apart from the enormous pay differential, in the United States the team was made up of engineers, 'silicon hackers', as Barron has described them. In England the people were mostly pure scientists, wanting the best, and in the American view forgetting that the best is often the enemy of the good. The Americans' scepticism and concern over the transputer's delays never, however, developed into outright hostility. But conflict was inevitable, for with Cheyenne Mountain having the only facility for producing batches of prototype chips for development purposes. American and British designs were bound to vie for priority.

As we shall see in a later chapter, the management policies adopted in the United States made the problem far worse and eventually began to affect the Cheyenne Mountain facility itself. Briefly, there was hardly any space for any kind of development work there for a period as all resources were concentrated on turning out current lines in as high volumes as possible.

It was not until the end of 1984, however, that such contention was to reach crisis point. Colorado was by then trying to debug the design of its latest memory, the cmos 64k static, just when the prototype versions of the transputer desperately needed processing. The problem was only to be finally resolved by setting up a prototyping line at Newport, where the 1985 chip slump had created spare capacity. So the transputer was finally to come home for the last stages of its development, but the transfer across the ocean imposed the last in a long series of delays. It is ironic that it was not until 1985 that the advantages of having a close relationship between design and manufacture, which had done so much to precipitate the traumas of 1980, were put into practice for Inmos's flagship British component.

Although it is still too early to say whether the transputer will turn out to be the worldbeater its British inventors conceived it to be, it is important to discuss the factors that will determine its chances. In a decade when high-technology industry has become increasingly demand-driven — listening to the needs of the marketplace rather than pushing its technology on reluctant users — one could argue that the transputer seems to be a throwback to an early era. If one accepts this premise, then the image of white-coated boffins sitting in a darkened room working out what people really need, rather than what they think they want, is hard to avoid in connection with the transputer. The 4004 had also been revolutionary, but at least it had been ordered by a customer. This is, of course, something of a caricature, but it is possible to draw parallels between the transputer and a whole host of British inventions that were scientific triumphs but commercial disasters.

The caricature could be grossly unfair and misleading. The ultimate aim of the whole Inmos project was, we should remember, to create a major semiconductor company. Starting from scratch in the late 1970s, Barron argued that the only possibility of achieving this was to take the high-risk options and attempt to innovate by creating new and exciting products in advance of the established opposition. In practical terms this meant being able to provide both memory and processing on a single chip by the early 1990s. Again, in practice, to make this ambition realisable, Inmos has no option but to turn itself into a major force in both memories and microprocessors. Now, it so happens that two giant United States corporations, Intel and Motorola, have the microprocessor market neatly stitched up between them. That is not to say that others do not make, and successfully sell, these parts in very large numbers, but the market is clearly dominated by the products of the two giants.

So Inmos had to find a way to break into the microprocessor business. The obvious route would have been to become one of those happily selling alongside the big two by producing a lookalike product that had a marginal performance advantage and hence finding itself a small niche. The second obvious alternative was to have become a second source for one of the established processor designs. In effect this would have meant making under licence and paying royalties on sales for a particular range.

It was not viable for Inmos to be a second source, as those who succeed here tend to have either specialist marketing or manufacturing skills they can bring to bear. One is, after all, competing with the original manufacturer. The one advantage a second source must have is that provided by a better sales force. Inmos did not have this advantage, nor an established base of its own customers to attack with a licensed technology. The problem with taking the first option and competing with a derivative of an existing architecture and a marginally better product has to do with Inmos's size and structure. It is a risky option, and those firms that succeed tend to be far larger than Inmos and well established in other chip markets. So, if Inmos wanted to succeed as a semiconductor house of international stature, Barron argued that its products would have had to be significantly different to those of the established competition. Such products would need to be significantly better on a variety of different technical criteria if they were to stand any chance against the established might of the big microprocessor houses.

Both Intel and Motorola have 32-bit processors of their own which hit the market at around the same time as the transputer. Inmos's and Barron's fervent hope is that because their part offers so much more than conventional designs and can be used to solve many more of a designer's problems than a conventional 32-bit processor, they will be able to grab a large part of the business created by the arrival of the next generation. The microprocessor trade is far less risky that the memory business, so if the transputer strategy works the company will have a far more secure base. Barron is confident that neither of the parts on offer from Intel or Motorola is nearly as well organised or technically executed as the transputer. Also because of their on-board memory and communications, transputers can be linked together to make computing engines of vastly superior power than anything else available, or likely to be available for sometime.

Another advantage with regard to the transputer is that the processor market has so far remained immune from attack by chip-makers from the Far East, which is more than can be said for memories. One reason for this is that the Japanese have taken a long time to develop a software base of sufficient sophistication to turn out good processor products. Barron also argues that the transputer does very definitely address market needs, but the gross needs of an expanding, technology-using community rather than the fiddly little needs of marginal improvements on existing components. So Inmos maintains that the transputer provides a great deal of power in a very small space. Users are also given access to a complex device that is nevertheless embedded in the simple system provided by occam. Once occam is understood, Inmos claims that it will be far easier to use the transputer to good effect.

There is no doubt that there is a great deal of enthusiasm for transputer chips in the market, but that does not necessarily infer that many people are going to buy them in large quantities. This is a point that Heightley recognised soon after he joined the company. The only real test of how well a product meets users' needs is the quantity bought. So conventional wisdom preaches that when planning a new device it is usually as well to base it on an existing product for which there is a known demand. The Inmos static rams, for example, were not revolutionary, but merely offered significantly better performance than rival but similar chips. Their sales were thus fairly well assured.

The transputer is such a risky venture, such a challenge, precisely because it is so radically different from anything that has gone before. If it succeeds it will be a triumph, but the odds have been against it from the start. It has done well to get this far, and certainly the chances of success will get better from now on. The technology judgement to which Inmos is now fully committed is that this route offered the only chance of breaking the American stranglehold on the microprocessor market. There is no doubt, in any case, that Inmos needs a broader product line than that offered by high-performance memory chips, and that it must develop a transputer, or something like it, if it is to live up to the promise of its business plan. Heightley was philosophical about the device.

If nothing comes out of the transputer project then we will have wasted a considerable investment. But by the standards of the microcomputer industry we have not spent that much on it and if we end up with a success, then we will have acquired it on the cheap.

Only time will tell which of Heightley's alternatives comes true.

There can be no doubt that from the time the Thatcher Government came to power it did not want Inmos to be state-owned. But it should be remembered that one of the principal concerns of the firm's founders during their original negotiations with the Labour Government in 1978 had been to secure a route by which the company could eventually become privately-owned. In the end, the NEB had presented the aim of a public share flotation, when the operation had become established, as a central part of the strategy. The prospect of a sell-off of the Government's majority holding had, as a result, been written into the first business plan despite heated opposition from the left of the Callaghan Government.

The policy the Conservatives had adopted did not therefore represent a departure from the plan, so long as they could be persuaded to wait until Inmos was properly established. Indeed, once the company could be seen to be successful, the presence of a Conservative tenant in Downing Street ought to have made its transition into the private sector easier to pull off. A Labour administration would have found itself with a nasty political row to sort out if it had tried to let a profitable Inmos go. But as things turned out, that was not one of the problems which fate had earmarked to torment Michael Foot.

Instead the Conservatives felt they had a different form of agony to endure. The £15 million of extra finance from the Government had been announced formally on 25 January 1983. Less then three months later, on 11 April, the new chairman, Sir Malcolm Wilcox, presented the firm's 1982 annual report and accounts. They made gloomy reading. Inmos had clocked up a loss of £20.4 million, during 1982, on sales of only £13.7 million

Most of the loss was generated by the firm's huge research and development costs and the expense of setting up Newport. The initial plan nevertheless stated that Inmos was to have had a turnover of £150 milion in 1984 and should have been able to finance growth from retained earnings after 1982. The £15 million cash injection and the thumping loss were the clearest evidence that the second of these objectives was not attainable and nobody, including Sir Malcolm, really believed that sales of anything like £150 million would be possible two years later in 1984. The official Inmos position was, however, that the figures were in line with the plan but running about a year behind schedule.

The delays were blamed, with condiserable justification, on the foot-dragging on the part of the Government in relation to granting the second £25 million tranche of scheduled investment and the extra costs associated with the positioning of the British plant. There had, of course, also been the technical problems that had put back the launch dates of the first products and between them, these problems had eaten up a great deal of extra cash. But Sir Malcolm, with his very limited experience of the semicoductor industry, could hardly have been expected to have known that technical delays are the rule rather than the exception with new chip-makers. All the same, when a company has a new fabrication plant and no well-established products to put into it and a second plant already half-built, perhaps even hardened semiconductor professionals might start to panic a little.

The City of London also had minimal experience in critically examining technology start-ups. Few there saw or understood the picture both Barron and Petritz wanted to portray − a picture of a company which had already demonstrated that it was able to design and deliver vlsi memories, one that was becoming well established in the 16k static ram business (by the time the report was presented Inmos was claiming 60 per cent of the world market), and one that had a portfolio of potentially highly credible future offerings. Instead the City saw a very high-risk business which was engaged in a project where the odds were stacked heavily against any entrant. Further, this entrant had just had to be given an unscheduled cash injection equivalent to 30 per cent of its initial equity, was under-performing relative to its own business plan, and had just turned in losses that on their own were guaranteed to frighten any financier. When combined with the estimated £50 million–£80 million of fresh investment that a resource-hungry Inmos was widely supposed to require during the following two years, Inmos was certain to scare away even the most entrepreneurial of fund managers.

The torment the Conservatives thus suffered was the thought of being lumbered with a technology start-up they could not abandon but which the City was not prepared to take off their hands. The publication of the figures in the spring of 1983 served to confirm the impression that had been acquired by potential investors when the Government had been searching in vain for alternatives to finding the £15 million extra funding itself. This exercise had been conducted during the second half of 1982. Even then sceptical investors had not been in the least interested, at least not at anything but a knock-down price which would have given them complete control of all of the firm's assets.

The mood was epitomised by the editorial stance of *The Economist*. In August 1982 it had used leaked information to produce a conclusion which with hindsight can be seen to be spectacularly wrong and at the time must have caused considerable damage. It stated:

> 'Inmos', the semiconductor company three-quarters owned by the government's high-technology holding company — the British Technology Group (BTG) — is on the scrounge for yet more money. BTG estimates that Inmos, which had already had £85 million from the taxpayer, will need another £10 million–£15

million next spring. Officially this is to cover a gap in its working capital. Unofficially, Inmos wants the loot to tart up its balance sheet into something the City could swallow without a liquid laugh.

It went on to doubt the viability of the markets for the company's major products and suggested that the BTG should be refused further funds for Inmos.

That *The Economist* knows an easy target when it sees it is hardly a revelation. After all, for years it has specialised in dressing up City orthodoxy to look cleverer than it really is. The interesting point is that since before the £15 million was agreed and Sir Malcolm came on the scene this orthodoxy had been opposed to offering Inmos any finance on realistic terms. All the same, when Sir Malcolm took the job of chairman he had been firmly told that the Government did not intend to provide any more money and he would have to find alternative sources to finance the business in future. Sir Malcolm had thus been set an impossible task by the Government's flat refusal to provide any more cash under any circumstances.

In effect, the firm's major shareholder had publicly stated that it was not prepared to support the company further, and would be making no more investments in it. Potential in-coming shareholders would therefore inevitably regard the British Government as a dead weight which was not prepared to support any of the future investment the company would have to make, and any new shareholders would have to carry the entire burden of finance themselves. This stance pre-sented Inmos as a prospect that was hardly attractive and certainly severely compromised the price the Government would get.

It was never made public exactly how difficult the job Sir Malcolm had taken on really was. The DTI and the BTG had reached a compromise over the future of Inmos with the Treasury and Downing Street. The DTI did not want to see the

company float away with its original majority shareholder having no say in its destiny, whilst the Treasury was adamant that it had to be neutralised as a financial liability. They agreed that Sir Malcolm would be instructed to find a private investor to come in alongside the Government. This investor should match the £15 million which the Government was itself providing and take some BTG equity in return. Even before the annual meeting in April 1983, this deal had been shown to be completely unworkable. Investors could not be found on terms that were remotely acceptable to either the company itself or the BTG. According to Barron, the very few candidates showing serious interest all demanded a majority stake for their £15 million. There were visits to Bristol by senior delegations from both Plessey and GEC during this period, say Inmos staff. It is also possible that other suitors confined their talks to BTG officials in London.

A further factor was not making Sir Malcolm's task any easier. Mrs. Thatcher's personal antipathy to the whole concept of Inmos was being widely reported at the time. She continually dismayed her advisers by deriding the company and its performance at every possible opportunity. 'Criticism like that upsets merchant bankers who know little about microchips,' complained one civil servant to *The Observer* at the end of January 1983. 'It certainly does not help us in the raising of private cash, a move which should be dear to her heart,' he added. It was a fairly desperate Sir Malcolm who told the annual meeting that spring that he would not rule out any particular route to increasing the spread of ownership. Nor would he rule out any route that lead straight to privatisation. To emphasise the point, he stated categorically that he would be looking at all of the possible alternatives with an open mind.

The start of the open season on Inmos had been declared. A wide variety of stories started to appear in the press alleging that a variety of foreign corporations, British companies and sundry technology entrepreneurs were keen to get hold of Inmos. None of these was ever officially denied by Inmos, which often genuinely did not know any more than it read in the papers about a particular overture. The BTG would never comment as it was afraid of jeopardising any talks that were actually in progress. Smoke screens and false trails could prove beneficial in this context. Indeed, the most improbable of stories was given at least superficial credibility by Sir Malcolm's declaration that he would be looking at any possibility, combined with the BTG's blanket no-comment policy. Some of the speculation was accurate, much of it was far from accurate, and most of it missed the crucial point that, with a few notable exceptions, all of those showing interest in Inmos were not interested in, or at least not being offered control of, the company. But at least for a while the DTI, Sir Malcolm, the BTG and the rest of Inmos's board were all pulling in the same direction.

After the abandonment of Sir Malcolm's first brief, to find £15 million worth of cash from a single punter to match the government's £15 million, a new policy was agreed. Three separate institutions — Inmos's own merchant bank, Hill Samuel, Lazards, which had been Inmos's advisers but was replaced when it started to work for the BTG, and the BTG itself — started a series of discussions in and around the City in an attempt to assemble a consortium to take a £15 million interest alongside the Government. Such a group was put together. It consisted basically of British financial institutions of various kinds, from the City and Edinburgh. The complication was that the group was not prepared to take part of the majority holding from the Government if it still refused to make any further investment. This group also insisted that an American investor who had experience with semiconductor technology and financial risks be found to join the consortium — 'smart money' in the jargon. The BTG steered around the first point and managed to stop the negotiations breaking down over the second by introducing a series of potential investors from the United States.

At this point the different interests involved started to pull in a variety of directions. The snag was that this was not the only initiative under way and the insistence by the British financial consortium that American money be involved focused attention on deep divisions in the Inmos board. These divisions reflected increasingly divergent views on the future of the operation. The tension was, as usual, most acute between the British and the American elements. At the start of 1983 the American stock market had fallen head over heels in love with high technology. Start-up firms with no track record, no products and little to recommend them beyond the, sometimes very considerable, reputations of the founders had managed to attract huge amounts of capital from public offerings. In February Monolithic Memories had netted $40 million, in March LSI Logic had got a record $143 million and in April Vti had managed a very useful $34 million.

None of this was lost on Inmos's American employees. Their feelings are well summed up by John Heightley:

> The discussions with the UK bankers and Hill Samuel about a private placement had started some time before, perhaps as long as a year. Nobody in the US could understand why we weren't going public when all of these others were doing it with no products, no billings, no anything. Hill Samuel seems to have known nothing about the American market and the advice we got was really terrible. The [US] employees thought we should be going public all through that period. Feeling in the corridors rose and fell to the same extent as the market. Each time it came down from a peak people felt another opportunity had been missed.

This feeling persisted within the American operation throughout 1983 and into 1984. Apart from the very high level of market interest in high-technology start-ups, the Americans saw the rest of the American semiconductor industry taking them progressively more seriously as the months went by. A respected source, the *ICE Review*, described Inmos as the fastest-growing semiconductor company ever recorded, and the exploratory talks Hill Samuel had already undertaken had involved some of the most prestigious names in the American technology trade who were interested in examining the business more closely.

All the same, much to the chagrin of the Colorado Springs end of Inmos, Hill Samuel advised that it was not practicable to go for a public offering in the United States. It pointed out that Inmos was not a start-up firm. It had been going for over four years, had clocked up big losses and was yet to turn in its first profit. Unlike the American start-ups, it was owned by the British Government which looked as if it was trying to dispose of its asset in double-quick time, at any price. These factors, it was felt, would inevitably be reflected in the amount an offering would raise. Merchant banking advice was also sought by Hill Samuel, and taken, in the United States, the consensus was that 1983 was not a good time to float the company. Apart from the considerations already mentioned, Sir Malcolm and the BTG seem to have been worried that American investors would not see why the sale was taking place. If all the bullish stories about Inmos were true, then why should the owner want to sell? It was feared that American investors might have become suspicious about the reasons for such a quick sale. The BTG would only have offered part of its holding to the American stock market and this might have in itself caused additional legal problems.

Furthermore, an American offering of even part of the stock would have caused a political row. The more successful an American flotation the more difficult it would have been to justify back home. A failure would be easier to live with politically but none the less embarrassing and would not have raised the cash; and fund-raising would have been the whole point of the exercise in the first place. Barron and the British side of Inmos did not want a placement of any of the BTG's holding in the United States during 1983. Inmos was started as a

primarily British company and that was the way they wished it
to stay. They had had four years to learn to deal with Whitehall,
and their initial innocence of the ways of bureaucracy was long
behind them.

Barron had already seen day-to-day control of the Newport
operation transferred across the Atlantic. All manufacturing
was now run directly from the United States and marketing also
reported straight to Colorado Springs. Only the design centre
was left under British control. In the months after Sir
Malcolm's arrival, the British operation seems to have been
fighting for survival. But, in retrospect, this period marked the
high point of American dominance. At the time there seemed a
real prospect that the firm was about to be taken over by its
American element, an event which the mooted share offering
in the United States would just have made more likely. On this
occasion at least, however, the embattled British managers
won. British Inmos had shrunk to a domain that ruled only
three floors of the Whitefriars office complex occupied by
Inmos in Bristol, but at least plans for an American public
offering had been thwarted. At Colorado Springs the staff
remained convinced that an American flotation was by far the
best route to secure the future financial needs of Inmos, and for
many of its employees to make a great deal of money.

Meanwhile, the consortium of financial investors in the
United Kingdom had run into problems. They had by this time
become very keen, the £15 million 'limit' had been exceeded
and over twice that amount offered. But the group's insistence
on bringing an American technology company with them
proved to be a stumbling-block. According to Barron, the
terms proposed were extremely onerous. The American
company involved — he refuses to reveal which it was —
would in effect have gained control of Inmos whilst having only
made a small part of the investment. The new Industry
Minister, Norman Tebbit, announced in the House of
Commons that the whole deal had fallen through. It looked at

the time as if the DTI had undervalued the company and belatedly realised the impractability of letting it go for so little. But in reality the Cabinet Office had objected strongly to the American investor's demand of securing its own nominees as board members and senior executives, since it believed that this would seriously disadvantage the existing major shareholder, the BTG.

The whole proposal was put completely out of court when the details of the conditions were examined. The Government would have retained responsibility for the loans and any debts stacked up by the company whilst handing over control. This cut right across the Treasury's prime objective: getting rid of something it regarded as a troublesome and expensive liability. The bringers of the 'smart money' seem to have thought they had a very strong position and could dictate terms: they had miscalculated. Now two initiatives in the United Kingdom had failed and Hill Samuel and the British part of the company had fought off any proposal for American flotation.

However, in June it was reported that Jack Tramiel, chief executive at Commodore, had been having talks in both the United States and Britain with Inmos executives, but these came to nothing. Barron says that GEC's Lord Weinstock made an appearance some time later in which he repeated the tactics he employed when offering to buy the company in 1981. GEC complained that it was interested in looking at the company, but that Inmos would not hand over any information on which it could make sensible decisions. A stream of reports appeared containing the complaint. *Technology* Magazine wrote of a

> fraught interchange between Inmos and GEC . . . Inmos became worried that GEC was asking far too much information about its future strategy, and GEC was miffed that it hadn't been able to get together a sensible offer. To make matters worse, there are persistent suspicions at Inmos that GEC simply wants to get at a fire sale price the parts of Inmos it wants . . . and absorb [them]

into its MEDL semiconductor operation, junking pet Inmos projects in the process.

Barron claims the truth is that there was no contact of any type:

> We eventually did give GEC some information but not until later. Weinstock was just trying to talk the price down. His posture was, as it had been in 1981, that we were not worth anything but if the BTG gave us away with 'adequate support' he would try and turn the company around.

When GEC eventually did get the information it had asked for, Inmos's prospects looked rather brighter than was the case in the spring of 1983. As the year progressed the two 16k static rams it had in production consolidated their hold on a market that was turning out to be very lucrative as the world-wide semiconductor industry neared the top of what was to prove a very strong cycle. On top of this, in June, the 16k by 4 64k dynamic ram had been launched. Its access time was very fast (100 nanoseconds) and the device looked as if it would be a strong contender for a good portion of the purchases of the classy and expanding high-resolution graphics products-makers and the booming personal computer suppliers. In August the world's fastest 16k static was launched by Inmos, consolidating its lead in the area. In July the occam-based system builder's workstation had been unveiled. The transputer itself was formally shown to the world in November and whilst few wanted to hold their breath until delivery day, there was much interest and well-informed applause. From the point of view of potential purchasers there was more evidence each month that the company was an attractive prospect.

All this had been predicted in the many presentations the company, its bankers and the BTG had been giving, but as time went on there was real evidence that the company was worth the risk that investors would have to take. The risk was still obviously high, but at least now potential investors could see for themselves that there was a plus side. Even *The Economist* had become a fraction less pessimistic. At one point during the year it had tried its hand at a spot of investigative journalism. '*The Economist* has discovered that many of the chips sold by Intel, and presumably bought by IBM, are in fact made by Inmos in its British plant and at its American factory in Colorado,' it reported approvingly one week.

GEC and Commodore apart, other companies also started to make very serious offers for the whole of the company. Many of the big American corporations that had been asked to join the first consortium came back independently, and AT&T had an offer on the table to take over the whole of Inmos. The problem was that the American telecommunications giant was only prepared to pay what Norman Tebbit described as a 'derisory £45 million'. AT&T had started looking at Inmos before the consortium was formed and had decided that it looked too attractive to leave to others. The corporation had obviously made a strategic decision that a good way to break into Europe would be by buying Inmos. It had also calculated that the British Government was sufficiently embarrassed to lack the will to reject a very low offer. The Government promptly did reject it but AT&T then came back with a series of revisions. All of these were well documented at the time, but many of those involved confirm that although AT&T tried to sweeten the pill in a variety of ways, including an offer to make research and development facilities available to Britain's leading computer maker, ICL, and a long list of manufacturing facilities they were prepared to set up in Britain, the one thing they would not move on was the very low price. It stayed at £45 million, all in.

The Government gave every sign of being extremely tempted by the final package offered by AT&T, and if it had been able to up its offer for Inmos, it is quite possible that the sale would have gone through. The British team were not totally happy with the offer but any opposition in the United Kingdom was overshadowed by the reaction of Inmos in the United States. They all were vehemently opposed. This was because AT&T had said that it proposed to close down Colorado Springs and move all of the people to AT&T sites. Barron recalls:

> I think our people in Colorado Springs were quite wrong. My analysis of the position was that AT&T had very little commercial experience or even practical technical expertise in semiconductor operations and in consequence many of the people in Inmos would quickly have risen to positions of control in AT&T technologies. From the point of view of the US team it actually represented a very good opportunity.

The American end of Inmos did not think so and as AT&T could not come up with a sum which the Government would accept, the whole issue became academic. Negotiations with AT&T continued almost until the day a sale was finally made. But in parallel with this option, other alternatives were also being explored.

After the collapse of the British investor consortium, work started on putting together a second group of investors. The crucial difference was that this time there was no question of buying out part of the Government's holding. The money raised would all be new money and new shares would be created. The Inmos directors were anxious that the existing shareholdings should not be diluted too much. So, although the investors were prepared to provide much more than the £15 million that Sir Malcolm had been told to find, the board tried to stop too much coming in.

Preparations were also going ahead for a public offering on the American stock exchange. Pressure from the American employees had become even stronger after the collapse of the consortium and in the autumn of 1983 Merrill Lynch had been taken on as American financial advisers. Unlike its predecessors, it saw an opportunity to float the company and gave appropriate advice. According to Heightley, the BTG 'was allowing us to spend $100,000's in preparations to go public'. The company was, for instance, as far back as November 1983, already conforming to the strict regulations the Securities and Exchange Commission in Washington demands from candidates for public offerings. Hence, for example, the Inmos public relations executives had to produce front covers of American magazines featuring previous Inmos products before the lawyers would give Inmos clearance to allow *Electronics* Magazine to print a cover shot of the transputer. The public relations executives also had to convince the lawyers that an announcement of a product that would not be available for at least eighteen months was really part of Inmos's 'normal course of business'.

Inmos employees in Britain were clearly still uneasy about a public offering in the United States but could do nothing to stop the preparations. They favoured the share deal that would have brought in a number of outside investors in Britain. Summing up the feelings of those in Bristol and Newport, Barron said:

> I think that if the company had gone public on the American market it would not have continued as the kind of company that the NEB invested in. We would have been a semiconductor company with a substantial operation in the US and an offshore plant in the UK. Undoubtedly the objectives of the original investors would not have been achieved. We would not have demonstrated that the UK can succeed in high technology.

Thus in early 1984 there was a race taking place. Either there would be a flotation in the United States, or the private placement of the specially created shares would go ahead in the United Kingdom.

As far as the British funding option was concerned, the American 'smart money' had by then been discarded; or, to be more accurate, those American investors who had shown interest had in most cases been directed towards the possibility of flotation in the United States, The British Government never formally denied the possibility of selling Inmos overseas. Subsequently Tebbit said that to have done so would have compromised the price obtainable from British companies. In combative mood whilst addressing the House, he told the Opposition that they were mad if they thought he would push down the price by excluding the Americans from the start.

No suitor ever seems to have been flatly turned down and the DTI can, in retrospect, be accused of running a rather unseemly auction with Inmos. And because no potential buyer or investor was ever told that even if they did come back with an improved offer it would still be turned down, the number of both hopeful purchasers and the remnants of their negotiating smoke screens that were still around during the first part of 1984 made sensible analysis by utsiders of what was going on very difficult.

The two main thrusts were, however, both going ahead. In the United States the public offering was well in hand and by late spring only weeks away. In Britain the private offering had been arranged. A group of investors had been assembled and a large company, Thorn EMI, had agreed to take a £10 million stake, giving it pole position in the group and boosting the confidence of the others. This deal would have secured the future of Inmos as an independent semiconductor house and, furthermore, would have given it some guarantee that the funds it would need for expansion would be available when wanted. The Americans were pushing ahead with the public offering at the same time.

In the end these two options were obviously far from compatible. Either a float on the American stock exchange, as Merrill Lynch had suggested, or the introduction of a group of private, British investors made good sense, but it was certainly not possible to do both without a fundamental restructuring of the company. None of the participants in the Inmos saga believed that both were likely to go ahead and had not therefore clarified the possible outcome. But it seems sensible to assume that in the unlikely event of both options being adopted, either there would have been a huge row at board level, with one faction coming out on top, or the company would have been broken into an American element and a British element, each being allowed to go its own way.

Inmos was British-owned, Sir Malcolm had said early on that his first instinctive reaction was to keep the company in British hands if he could, and the British management was heavily opposed to falling any further under the power of the American semiconductor industry. So, barring a hitch at the last moment, it seems most probable that the group of private British investors would have become the new controllers of Inmos's future. But it would have been hard to persuade the American management to welcome this outcome.

The Americans may have thought that the group of private investors were doomed to the same fate as the earlier consortium, in which case the American flotation would have been the only remaining alternative. And there were abundant rumours at this time that Petritz was still seeking loan capital to finance a buy-out of the American operation. But it never came to a showdown.

At the beginning of July 1984 the directors of Inmos were informed that all existing deals were off. A buyer had been found for Inmos: Thorn EMI was to take over the whole business outright for £95 million. Was it a sensible, if surprising, sell-off or a spineless sell-out? To find an answer we need to look at the new owner.

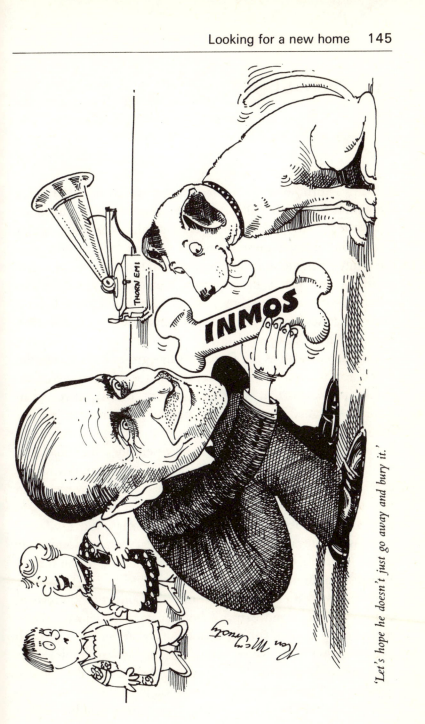

'Let's hope he doesn't just go away and bury it.'

11   Thorn Steps Forward

Before Thorn EMI bought Inmos, electronic products accounted for nearly half of the overall turnover of this long-established British conglomerate. But the vast bulk of its electronic turnover came from sales of consumer products in the United Kingdom, its home market. Thorn was not the first electrical and electronic equipment maker to discover the potential of microelectronics. In fact, it had lagged behind many of its competitors in adapting its offerings to the new horizons that had opened up.

Companies such as the Dutch Philips group had, during the 1960s, for example, started to appreciate the implications of the technical changes that were taking place and had invested in facilities designed to safeguard its international competitiveness. At that time Thorn seemed to believe that the relatively low-technology metal-bashing and hand-assembly which made up the bulk of its activities faced no real threat. Then, during the early 1970s, Thorn's own international competitiveness had taken a very severe battering. This served, at least partially, to push it out of its complacency, and Thorn found itself at a particular disadvantage because its factories were predominantly in the United Kingdom, with a few to be found in the former British dominions.

As the British exchange rate moved against the interests of British exporters and British labour costs rose, Thorn became increasingly dependent on a home market which was itself under growing pressure from cheap, yet technologically sophisticated, imports. The adverse exchange rate also focused attention on the far more serious problem of the fast declining market appeal of many of Thorn's consumer durables in the face of more up-to-date competitive products. And the rise in the cost of labour highlighted the very high labour content of the firm's wares, compared to their overseas equivalents. Most long-established British manufacturing businesses could, and often have told similar stories. All the same, Thorn had managed to make some spectacular profits from the colour television business, even if the markets it had helped create in Britain and Europe for televisions and other medium technology consumer products had begun to shrink badly.

The company had been founded by Sir Jules Thorn, one of the pioneers of the British television and fluorescent tube industries. Soon after the take-over of Inmos, the American magazine *International Management* said of the late Sir Jules that he 'demanded and received unquestioning loyalty from devoted but underpaid managers as he built Thorn into the largest television rental organisation in the world, backed by the Ferguson production lines'. After Sir Jules's retirement as chairman in 1980, the company started to look for higher technology options. This undoubtedly made good sense for Thorn but was hardly sufficient to qualify it as the ideal new owner for such a high risk and extremely demanding venture as Inmos.

Whilst Thorn's profit margins on its traditional products were under increasing pressure, the firm's management looked enviously at GEC, Racal and Plessey, companies where life was apparently made far easier by their heavy reliance on military business with its fixed margins, low volumes and guaranteed sales. Harold Mourgue, Thorn's financial director for many years and later deputy chairman, candidly admitted that as Thorn found it harder to earn sufficient margins on traditional lines, a move into military technology seemed to offer a tempting way out.

Indeed, such a move would have formed the basis of a perfectly sound business strategy. For a British company involved in the technology sector in almost any form the safest and surest route to survival is to become involved with military contract work. We have touched on this issue before, and will return to it again. For the moment it is enough to say that any British-based company that keeps to the general rule of always developing and chasing military contracts when the chance arises will find its relationships with the City much easier and will pay less for its borrowings. Its managers will also be almost universally regarded as custodians of a more worthy and better-run enterprise than would be the case if it were more dependent on civilian products.

Thorn thus decided that it wanted to emulate the pattern so well exemplified by GEC by expanding into the (for it) new and highly profitable areas of military technology. At the same time, as a secondary objective, it realised that some provision had to be made to provide its existing products with a secure supply of microelectronic parts, design and manufacturing advice, and know-how.

The traditional Thorn empire, before any new lines were added, consisted of a sprawling collection of enterprises. It spread across such disparate areas as the highly profitable television rental business: Radio Rentals, the Rumbelows chain of high-street consumer durable sellers, and home appliance manufacture under the Kenwood, Bendix and Tricity labels. The Ferguson television manufacturing plants and Britain's largest lighting business were still in the portfolio, and a telecommunications business had been added early on through a joint venture with the Swedish firm Ericsson. Thorn–Ericsson, however, had remained a minor telecommunications supplier until it won an important contract to supply main telephone exchanges to British Telecom during 1985.

Thorn had purchased the whole of the EMI company after the retirement of Sir Jules. With this deal it acquired a highly respected central research laboratory, which had spawned a Nobel Prize winner and a few high-technology, if not particularly profitable, businesses. It also became a major record manufacturer both in the United Kingdom and the United States and a music publisher of international stature. Through EMI it also became the owner of the ABC chain of cinemas and a 46 per cent stake in Thames TV. Mourgue said of the firm's philosophy in the early 1980s:

> If you are ever going to have anything that other people haven't got you are going to have to start getting into this whole chip thing. Because the chips are taking over the design of the actual circuitry. It is as true of dishwashers and washing machines as it is of televisions.

So, six months before Thorn paid out £95 million for Inmos, it was seriously considering finding itself an involvement in the semi-custom chip business. Semi-custom chips, it will be remembered, are devices that have been partially tailored to a specific application in a particular environment or piece of equipment. They are most often found in the kind of product made by companies such as Thorn, where volumes are high but production runs not sufficiently long to justify the costly process of designing a special chip from scratch. On the other hand, considerable savings can be made by having something more specialised than a standard microcircuit, which has to be specially programmed and usually requires a variety of additional circuits to make it work.

It would have been possible for Thorn to find a number of candidates roughly meeting its requirements in the United Kingdom. The problem was that none of them was up for sale. Most belonged to the large British military technology contractors which had all kept an involvement with semi-custom circuit technology as it was increasingly used in many military and telecomminications systems during the 1970s. A semi-custom chip designer and manufacturer was precisely what Inmos was not. Indeed, the original idea behind the project had been to import into the United Kingdom the capacity to make the kind of high-volume standard chips that the indigenous British companies like GEC, Plessey and Racal had decided to abandon, or eschew, in favour of their military contracts a decade before.

In the intervening period, however, chip technology had changed sufficiently to render semi-custom chips into a viable route to use in order to inject electronic sophistication into some of the electrical and electronic consumer goods Thorn was already making. Thorn was therefore increasingly on the look-out for a way of gaining access to an application-specific chip process. The options available were to seek a partnership or acquire an already-established design and/or manufacturing firm. A take-over would, however, have had to have been fairly cheap as this was only a minor part of the overall strategy. Most of the funds Thorn had available for expansion had been earmarked for the move into the lucrative military arena, where the only significant customer was the Government and the vagaries of consumer tastes were eliminated.

During the first part of 1984 almost all of the energies of the senior management of Thorn were directed towards the prospect of purchasing British Aerospace (BAe), when they were not involved in the running of the company itself. Thorn under its recently recruited boss, Peter Laister, had set itself firmly on a path of realising its ambitions by merging with BAe. Contrary to popular opinion, the civil aircraft side of BAe represented only a small part of the planemaker's activities, accounting for only about one-eighth of its turnover. Much of its dominant defence-oriented business was electronic in nature and on the whole BAe was just the kind of military contractor Thorn wanted in its stable. Before launching its bid, Thorn had undertaken extensive research on BAe's activities and prospects. The same cannot be said of its knowledge of Inmos.

There was in fact some direct contact between the two organisations through Sir William Barlow, who was one of Inmos's non-executive directors appointed by the Government and at the same time deputy chairman at Thorn, alongside Mourgue. But, according to a variety of sources, Sir William was careful to keep his different responsibilities in separate compartments. He did let the Thorn mandarins know how Inmos was progressing in the most general of terms. When he had first joined the Inmos board, much of what he reported back was highly critical, but as time went on, and Inmos's immediate financial prospects brightened, so his reports became more enthusiastic. So when Thorn was approached with a view to joining the group that was being assembled to buy the new shares in Inmos, it showed considerable interest.

Thorn did not believe Inmos represented the kind of investment that would provide the mainstream involvement in the military market it wanted, but it did hope to do a deal with Inmos whereby a semi-custom facility would be built with Thorn money and run by Inmos staff. Mourgue says the discussions on this point were only exploratory and of the most general kind, but Thorn felt sufficiently encouraged to agree in principle to becoming an industrial partner for the group of financial institutions that were forming up to take a minority stake in Inmos.

BAe would have taken most of the funds Thorn had to play with, but the group's share price had gone sky-high at the start of 1984 and in consequence it had a great deal of money readily available for investment. Thorn therefore felt that it could afford a share of the £15 million stake in Inmos and still be able to take on the far larger BAe. There was no formal commitment to Inmos but it looked highly likely that the minority stake would be taken up.

Given that Inmos was not a semi-custom chip-maker, and had no desire to become one, its strategic relevance to the Thorn portfolio was therefore limited. But Thorn was brimming over with money at the time and its most senior managers had a strong desire to make it a bigger force in the technology game. Even if Inmos did not fit Thorn's needs very well, it could hardly have gone far wrong by taking only such a modest stake in the chip-maker.

One of Laister's first actions when he took over was to ask for a series of reports with recommendations for ways of making the group less vulnerable in the 1990s. It was as a result of this exercise that the BAe take-over scheme was born. It was not, however, the only corporate development proposal seriously canvassed. Douglas Stevenson, for example, had come to Thorn three years before Laister as a part-time consultant on high technology and had recommended a very different strategy with a far heavier emphasis on mainstream electronics than the BAe option provided for.

Thorn made its bid for BAe in April 1984. Between then and mid-June this bold move took up all of the attention of the Thorn management. But both BAe management and the City failed to see the logic of the merger and were hostile right from the start. So, inevitably, the bid failed and, suddenly, Thorn found that the main foundation stone of its strategy was built on sand. Laister's personal reputation in the City took a big knock, from which it never recovered. While the speed with which the scheme had appeared had taken many of the City institutions by surprise, its sudden disappearance made the episode appear a fiasco to even more and Laister took most of the blame.

From the point of view of Inmos, the abandonment of the BAe project turned out to be of great significance. The Thorn management sat down to review collectively the remains of its tattered strategy. During the BAe episode a few managers in the Thorn hierarchy had argued that taking a bigger stake in Inmos represented a better investment than BAe. They had been overruled at the time but once the larger deal had irrevocably failed the issue was examined again.

Inmos might have been smaller than BAe and the notoriously volatile chip business might have looked very different to the safe, complacent, rich world of government contract work, but Inmos did certainly get its share of lucrative military business. Most 16k static rams, a business that it dominated, were destined for military systems of one kind or another and the transputer had enormous implications for military research programmes. In their gloomier moments the Bristol design team feared that the initial wave of transputer customers would be military research establishments; few civilian outfits had the size of budget to exploit the revolutonary chip's potential without special funding.

The eventual purchase of more than a £10 million stake in Inmos was, by all accounts, carried out in an unseemly rush. Douglas Stevenson, a former corporate vice president and group executive of ITT's component and semiconductor operations, only found out that Thorn intended to buy the whole of Inmos when he got off a plane after a visit to Japan, by which time it was public knowledge. Stevenson was Thorn's main semiconductor expert so his lack of knowledge of the impending purchase is the strongest possible evidence of the haste with which the sale was arranged and the extent to which it was a leap in the dark for Thorn.

The BTG and the Inmos board knew, of course, of Thorn's interest in taking a minority holding and for Barron and some of the other Britons this represented the preferred route to privatisation. News of the offer by Thorn to buy a majority stake outright came, however, not from the company but directly from the Government. The offer was kept a close secret almost until the Inmos board was officially informed that all the plans they had been working on had been scrapped and that the Government intended to sell its entire shareholding to a single buyer.

Sir William was surprisingly not involved in the acquisition, despite having a foot in both camps. In fact, he is said by Barron to have lost money because of the speed with which the purchase was pushed through — more evidence of the hastiness of the transaction. Barlow apparently exercised his Thorn share purchase options, to which his position as deputy chairman entitled him, just before the share price tumbled from its high point as a result of the City's adverse reaction to the Inmos take-over.

For the Government the Thorn deal represented an ideal opportunity for it to get its money back, save face and remove from its books the potential liability that the Treasury still saw in Inmos. It was the Treasury that had consistently pushed for a sale that would completely end the state's financial responsibility. Under either of the funding schemes favoured by the factions inside Inmos itself, the Government would still have had to honour its loan guarantees and would possibly have been called upon to make further investments.

Thorn also provided the Government with a presentable outcome enabling Mrs. Thatcher and Norman Tebbit to hold their heads up high in the House of Commons and maintain that they had done the best thing possible for the company. Although the Government got a good price for Inmos — £95 million in cash from Thorn which also took over £35 million of loan guarantees — the sale did contradict the statements individual Conservative ministers had occasionally made about the need to foster and develop in Britain more highly motivated, high-technology companies that were free from the bureaucratic constraints of established big business (the implication often being that in the case of large, established British companies the problem was more acute than with their overseas counterparts).

Inmos had surely become exactly the sort of operation many Conservatives wanted to see created in large numbers. Yet the taint of state funding which hung over Inmos, and the expediency of getting rid of responsibility for a potential financial liability for many years to come, overwhelmed any qualms they may have had about damaging the chances of such a potentially good example of dynamic free enterprise. Thorn was, after all, in the private sector, and even if it would have been more creative to allow Inmos to continue as an independent entity, surely, they argued, it could not fail to flourish in the harsh but invigorating climate of the free market.

In contrast to this view, Heightly, along with many of the Americans employed by Inmos, maintained that the take-over of the company by any large commercial organisation, and its consequent loss of independence, would be bound to eat out the entrepreneurial heart from Inmos before it reached its full potential. He cited some impressive evidence from the experience of other semiconductor houses that have been sold to big companies to back up this claim. In general, the subsequent performance of chip-makers that have become subsidiaries of large companies has been at best reasonable. At worst it has been disastrous.

Synertek, for example, was set up in 1973 and five years later was bought by the American Computer company, Honeywell. In 1985 it went bust. Yet Signetics became part of Philips and has prospered. In between these two extremes Zilog, which was bought by Exxon, and Inmos's old adversary Mostek, acquired by United Technologies, are both believed to have become financial burdens for their new owners. More recently, Gould has taken a majority stake in AMI and in Europe the American/ French joint venture, Eurotechnique, was incorporated into the giant nationalised French Thomson Group. It is too early to judge how well either has faired, but Thomson was known to be investing £140 million in its semiconductor operations in 1985 with the aim of achieving profitability within two years. It is obviously possible to make very different judgements about each of these takeovers, and wide or sweeping generalisations about such a diverse group would be unfair. But it does seem that the prognosis for a semiconductor house that comes under the wing of a big corporation is none too bright.

The Department of Trade and Industry in London knew this

all too well when the fate of Inmos was being decided. According to our investigations, its senior civil servants were strongly in favour of the British chip-maker staying free from the embrace of any large company. It is a measure of the weakness of the DTI in the face of pressure from the Treasury with backing from Downing Street that Inmos was not allowed to go and find its own finance, with the Government remaining in the background as a guarantor of its continued freedom.

Instead, the decision was taken to talk Laister into taking it as a consolation prize in the wake of Thorn's failure to acquire BAe. For the speed at which the deal was transacted had not been determined by Laister. He probably would have liked to take things more slowly, although some of those closely involved in the proceedings later maintained that this was not the case, but the Government was pushing hard for the sale to be completed as soon as possible.

Thus the timing of the purchase was not of Thorn's choosing. Indeed, from its point of view it could hardly have been worse. Thorn had already planned a rights issue to cash in on its high share price on the Stock Exchange. The original plan had been to go ahead with the rights issue and then a few days later to announce the use to which the money was to be put, namely, the purchase of Inmos. But the Government insisted that the sale should be completed before the Secretary of State, Norman Tebbit, was due to speak in the House about Inmos. This speech was fixed for Thursday, 12 July 1984.

The Government also demanded cash on the nail in exchange for Inmos. As Thorn needed the funds raised by the rights issue to pay for Inmos, it could hardly postpone its fund-raising exercise. Besides, the first available alternative date would have been about five weeks later since the Stock Exchange operates a waiting list for such ventures. Thorn was therefore forced to launch its issue on Tuesday, 17 July, just four days after the announcement by Tebbit in the Commons. Thorn's share price crashed, as its financial advisers had predicted. Inmos thus cost the group an enormous amount and the share price had not recovered by the start of the dramatic decline in the value of electronics stocks in the spring of the following year. Yet again it was Laister who was blamed by the City for what it saw as bungled timing.

Thorn might have been railroaded by the Government into a quick buy, but the negotiations were nevertheless time-consuming because of the complex capital structure of Inmos. The Government imposed deadline meant that the talks went on late into the night at the DTI offices in Victoria Street. The BTG only held 76 per cent of the shares. The rest were with the employees, but the structure had been planned to preserve the BTG's control even if it sold some of its holding. Thorn wanted to ensure that it was gaining control of the company. The employee shareholders were keen to get a return on their holdings, and Thorn was obliged by Stock Exchange rules to offer them at least as good a price as it paid the Government, which meant that Petritz, Schroeder and Barron were set to become very wealthy men. The £15,000 investment each had made back in 1978 was now worth about £6 million. Others in the company had smaller holdings that were now worth many thousands. There were 280 employee shareholders who had taken equity at the rate it had been offered in the early days and others had been able to take options later.

Thorn was naturally keen to discourage the Inmos employees, its greatest asset, from just taking the money and running. Those in the American operation in particular, who had been dismayed by the sudden decision to sell to a British corporation, were thought to be especially at risk. One effect of the take-over had been to ensure that the company would never fall into American hands and those who had pushed for a flotation in the United States would have had good reason to feel let down. Schroeder, for example, who had left the company three years before, took up the offer and cashed in his holding.

A formula was eventually worked out by which Thorn would create incentives to encourage the 'high flyers' to stay on and not cash in their holdings. Those who elected to stay were given an annual series of dates after which their shares would have a value determined by the average annual revenues of the company. During the semiconductor boom of 1984, this seemed to be guaranteeing a higher future price than the £18 the Government had acquired. As most of the employees were not particularly well off, they were, despite the formula, tempted to cash in at least part of their holdings to give themselves a little spare cash. This reason applied with the greatest force to those in the British Inmos operation. The first offer closed in January 1984 and when Thorn revealed the results a few weeks later, as it was bound to do under Stock Exchange rules, it was shown to have 82.9 per cent of the Inmos stock. So, after the first offer it was evident most of the 280 worker shareholders, with the exception of Schroeder, had hung on to their shares.

A year later, however, the incentive formula started to work against Thorn and forced it to buy far more shares than it would have liked. Because the price the staff shareholders would get was determined by Inmos's average profits over a number of years, the traumatic chip slump of 1985 seemed certain permanently to depress the formula offer price. There was a rush to cash in before the beneficial effects of the 1984 boom on the price were negated by the disappointing sales of the following year.

The formula was badly constructed from the start. Nobody who had more than a rudimentary understanding of the cyclic nature of the semiconductor industry would expect the kind of growth rate that Inmos had experienced in 1983/84 to be sustained. Semiconductor companies just do not behave in that way. They are part of a highly volatile and fast-moving business where the profits can be huge in the short term for the succesful few. Those who do not get it right will usually survive to try again when the next business cycle or wave of technological change throws all participants back to the starting-gate. Firms will survive and prosper, therefore, only if they are both lucky and well managed.

A share incentive scheme that relies on steady, sustained growth for its incentives to operate is thus of completely the wrong design to work in a semiconductor company. It is hardly surprising that such a scheme did not work too well in the case of Inmos. Yet this failure seemed to come as a big surprise to Thorn. The share purchase formula had, however, only been devised as a holding operation until a public flotation of part of the Inmos stock could be arranged by Thorn. But as Thorn, in the light of the City's hostility and the chip depression, delayed this on numerous occasions some despaired that it would ever happen and decided to take the cash when the deal seemed better than it would ever likely to be for some years.

Some of those who had decided to take the money had good reason to know that Inmos's results following its 1984 success were going to look far worse than an ordinary downturn in the market by itself could be expected to produce. This, too, as we shall see, was also unexpected by Thorn. None of which detracts from the fact that in the summer of 1984 Thorn had brought itself a first-class chip company, even if it had not acquired the reliable and close source of semi-custom chips for its own products that it had originally set out to obtain.

Thorn might not have been too clear of what use Inmos was going to be in the short term, but it is illuminating to look at the plans the company said it had for its new acquisition just after the take-over. Mourgue, who became the new Thorn-appointed, part-time chairman of Inmos, said soon after the take-over that the transputer had been of real interest and that Thorn had faith in its future. Mourgue had also acknowledged and supported Inmos's strategy of being a high-performance, high value-added chip-maker addressing large niche markets. So although all of the Thorn management had reservations about being involved in the fiercely competitive dynamic ram business, Inmos had successfully pointed out that without the educational value of dram production it would not have been possible to develop and make the technically very advanced products it was working on.

So, by early 1985 the new parent had committed itself to providing a minimum of £20 million for the first two years after the take-over, and as the full consequences of the appalling 1985 slump were realised, this commitment was believed to have been doubled. As the semiconductor industry often talks in terms of investment levels of around 25 per cent of turnover, even the latter figure seemed not over-generous and insufficient to fund the building of any more fabrication facilities in the near future.

Towards the end of 1984 and into 1985 it was slowly dawning on Thorn executives exactly what they had got themselves into. The company did not know much about semiconductors and it had not bothered to consult Stevenson, its only real expert, before buying Inmos. No one in Thorn carried out any serious research on chip markets or on the possible future links with parts of Thorn. No Thorn manager had troubled to go and see Inmos's executive directors and talk to them about the problems of coordinating a company with sites and staff on both sides of the Atlantic and how they had tried to overcome the inevitable conflicts between the different parts. If Thorn managers had taken these elementary precautions they may well have discovered that Inmos was rather worse prepared to meet the rigours of the downturn than it might have been.

Whilst the company had been preparing for the initial public offering on the American stock market, the option strongly favoured by its American employees in general and by Petritz and Heightley in particular; all of its operations had been run from the United States. For the public offering to be the runaway success the United States hoped for, the trading figures needed to be as good as possible. To this end, all of the operational resources at the disposal of the American managers had been devoted to turning out as many 16k statics, Inmos's best sellers, as was possible. The Americans can hardly be blamed for making a semiconductor outfit efficient at making semiconductors, but they were blamed for what Thorn saw as corner-cutting on quality standards and for devoting all of the production facilities to current products at the expense of any development work.

At one point the transputer team could not get any of its silicon processed through the production-lines because they were permanently engaged in memory production. And, without production runs to process new versions the transputer development programme became bogged down. Exactly the same delays were being imposed on Inmos's other new product developments, and few designs were getting through to the pre-production phase. Stevenson, who had eventually been appointed to the Inmos board as a non-executive director, described this procedure as 'eating the seedcorn'.

Of course, from the point of view of Petritz and Heightley this was a gamble worth taking. Their main objective, it must be remembered, was for the company to achieve a successful flotation on the American stock market. Obviously, the better they could make the latest trading figures appear, the more demand there would be for the firm's shares at the time of the initial public offering. And even after the Thorn purchase they continued with this policy; Thorn after all was publicly committed to offering a portion of the equity on the open market.

This management stance was not, however, calculated to endear Petritz and Heightley to Thorn. By pushing as much silicon as possible out of the doors of the fabrication plants when times were good, problems were only being stored up for the future. Not only would there be a longer lag than otherwise would have been needed to get replacement products on to the market, but the company would in all likelihood require extra support during the downturn.

With the benefit of hindsight it is easy to criticise the American managers but, in fairness, it should be realised that they had no more idea than anyone else in the industry just how bad the 1985 slump was to turn out to be. It is also axiomatic that, for any semiconductor company, the bigger its sales during the boom portion of the semiconductor cycle, the more products it should expect its customers to attempt to return when the cycle turns down.

When chips are scarce, users will go to almost any lengths to secure their supplies; they will sign agreements for delivery way into the future, if it will get them out of a supply crisis in the short term. They will also grossly over-order. When demand for their products slackens not only will they stop ordering from the semiconductor houses, they will take all practical steps to reduce their stock of chips, including returning stock to suppliers where there has been some degree of reliability problem.

Unfortunately for Petritz and Heightley, Inmos's customers had been given ample opportunity to find fault with some of the products that had been turned out of the company's plants during 1984 and for the first part of 1985. During the autumn of 1984 the monthly report Heightley made to the board back in the United Kingdom started to contain references to production problems with the memory lines. Such problems are by no means rare in the business; the yield from some fabrication plants in Silicon Valley has been known to drop from 70 per cent to nothing virtually overnight. Neither is it uncommon for the technologists in charge to be unable to pinpoint an immediate cause.

The tolerances in the chip production game are very tight. A few small irregularities in a number of stages can easily accumulate to generate faulty products. Monthly reports from operational directors of fabrication plants are full of such references. The feature that made the Inmos reports in late 1984 unusual was that Thorn at last started to take some notice.

Heightley talked of contamination by mobile ions and problems with metalisation.

Some of the twenty-five or so stages of producing a semiconductor memory involve embedding ions of obscure elements at various levels in the structure of the chip and then allowing them to diffuse through it. But stray ions can also be introduced by accident. The most common cause is when the production process is slightly slack and all of the rigorous clean-room procedures are not being strictly adhered to. The real nightmare for the producers comes when ions migrate inside the complex structure and create a switch in an unpredictable place. Worst of all, the manufacturer's test procedures may not pick up the fault if the ions concerned take time to migrate to a position where they impair the function of the whole chip. When this happens a producer can have shipped large quantities of faulty chips which would all have to be recalled to the factory.

More often the faults are not too drastic, but during the slump users keen to dump surplus stocks have a habit of crying wolf. It is a brave fabrication plant manager who can maintain for ever that there is no possibility of faulty product ever having left his plant. Sometimes chips that are known to have contained some minor faults are unknowingly shipped. If the faults do not show up, except under the most sophisticated testing procedures, the chips concerned will be perfectly adequate for most applications. And when demand is high there is a strong temptation for fabrication managers to ignore minor imperfections in their plant's products. In Inmos's case in 1983/84 this temptation was reinforced by the need to make the sales figures look as attractive as possible. For whatever reason, slack production procedures and management, or deliberate shipping of slightly risky products, Thorn found itself with a nasty and potentially embarrassing quality problem on its hands by the end of 1984.

This kind of thing is likely to happen to any semiconductor

house. The problem is not uncommon, and will pass over in the end with the only likely consequence being for the company to have to take as returns some chips that under different circumstances the customers would have been perfectly happy to keep. But Thorn did not know this. Thorn was suddenly faced with an urgent need to make financial provision for large quantities of returned product to Inmos. As the semiconductor recession deepened it also became obvious that Inmos was going to need far more cash to see it through than Thorn had originally budgeted for. The good times of 1984 were going to be turned into what could in all probability be a loss in 1985. On top of all of this Thorn was discovering that owning a competitor in the chip business can be an expensive pastime. The levels of investment required just to keep technology and manufacturing equipment up to date are, for example, massive.

It all started to look too much to bear. Thorn had other problems with the television manufacturing part of its empire, where very heavy financial losses and subsequent major redundancies were looming. Thorn was set to go from being massively cash-rich, as a result of its high share price in the summer of 1984, to badly in trouble with the market just a year later. And it was to be Laister's head that went on the block. The Inmos acquisition had always been unpopular with the City and now hostile financial institutions had even more reason to devalue Thorn further.

In the spring of 1985 Stevenson was appointed as the new chief executive and Heightley was demoted from his role as chief operations officer for the entire company but retained direct responsibility for Colorado Springs. Stevenson intended to manage the British end of Inmos himself. But things were not to remain like this for long. On 1 July 1985, Thorn announced that Laister had resigned as chairman and chief executive of Thorn to be replaced by Sir Graham Wilkins, a non-executive director who had little direct experience of running a large technology company. Colin Southgate, Thorn's managing director, stayed on and moved closer to overall day-to-day control of the firm.

The main reason for the coup was given by the new Thorn regime as being the very bad interim financial results they were due to announce on 5 July. Inmos was blamed as a major contributor to the company's poor performance. The figures showed that Thorn was making a £20 million financial provision for returns of faulty Inmos chips. The Inmos management, including Stevenson, were appalled by Southgate's statements at the meeting to announce the figures and the special provisions.

It was a massive blow to the market credibility of Inmos's static memory products. Further, it revealed considerable *naivete* about the realities of the chip business. Thorn even threatened to ask the Government to return some of its money for the purchase, claiming that it had not been made aware of all of the circumstances surrounding the company when it was for sale. It was true that Thorn knew very little about Inmos when it bought it; it had only itself to blame, but Laister had been the scapegoat. Meanwhile, as the problem grew, Petritz and Heightley were forced, with some justification, to share the blame and they were relieved of all executive responsibility. A few days later both resigned.

According to Stevenson, Heightley had come up with a plan, when the semiconductor recession first hit, to close the Newport plant to save funds whilst leaving the American operation very much intact. The plan also meant that there would be no possibility of getting transputer silicon procesed in Colorado, prolonging even more the delay in this crucial part's introduction. Barron told Stevenson that if the plan went ahead then the Bristol design team would fall apart. Thorn would then have been left with little more than a shell in the UK; the viable parts of the American operation would have quickly drifted out of its control. The Heightley plan was rejected and he and Petritz, the man who created the whole Inmos idea, severed their contacts with the company.

Theirs were not the only jobs to go. Around 500 people, a third of the overall work-force, were to lose their jobs in Stevenson's alternative plan to deal with the chip recession. The redundancies were to fall equally on both the Inmos factories. Newport was to be dedicated to the production of the transputer, whilst Colorado Springs was to concentrate on production of high-speed memories. Mourgue, who stayed on as Inmos chairman during the crisis, told reporters that Inmos needed to cut costs by $20 million. The redundancies, he said, were going to occur throughout the company, involving executives as well as production workers. And, as it turned out, many of the sacked executives came from the United States.

During the purge, all attempts to float off the American end of the business were to be firmly stopped. Barron would stay on at Bristol to develop the transputer, which would be produced in Newport under Stevenson's control, whilst Colorado Springs would make static rams. The company obviously had to do something drastic to meet the financial crisis the semiconductor slump had precipitated. But it got a very rough deal by being caught up in the internal political struggles at Thorn. Perhaps the new men at Thorn were painting things blacker than they really were in order to be able to reveal some kind of miraculous transformation a few months later. Certainly, however, Thorn was showing that its very worrying lack of understanding of competitive chip-making had led it into disaster. In any case, Inmos had always had sufficient internal political battles of its own to fight without having to bother about those of others. The struggle over control of the plants and the future of the transputer were sufficient to keep all of the Inmos participants happy for a long time without the added complication of Laister's rivals using the problems of Inmos as a weapon in the battle to unseat him.

Whatever the hypothetical advantages of Inmos remaining independent with a minority private owner, the wholesale take-over of the company by Thorn seemed, at least, to confer one immediate and lasting benefit: stability. For years a victim of political indecision and interference, the company had apparently acquired a single permanent owner with straight-forward, if ill-defined, aims. And the new regime got off to a good start. Cashing in on the 1984 chip boom, mostly fuelled by the phenomenal growth of personal computing. Inmos was able to announce proudly in February 1985 that it had made profits of £14.4 million on record sales of £110.8 million. It had captured 27 per cent of the world-wide static ram market — more than all the American suppliers put together.

It was generally accepted that the minimum investment needed to set up a commodity chip-maker had, by 1984, jumped to $150 million, far more than Thorn paid for a going concern. Evaluated on the same criteria as other semiconductor start-ups in the United States in the boom days of 1984, Inmos would have had a market value of £518 million, more than four times the Government's selling price.

But Thorn's perception that it had got itself a bargain was, as we have seen, not to last for very long. The sales estimates, and chip orders, of the personal computer makers proved wildly over-optimistic and, coupled with the normal cyclical downturn in the industry, this plunged the semiconductor business early the following year into its deepest-ever recession. But, for a while at least, Thorn had kept its nerve. Its managers had had six months to familiarise themselves with the arcane workings of the chip business, and had learned the painful lesson that semiconductor makers must continue to invest when business is bad if they are to stand a chance of cashing in on the next boom.

Thorn had cautiously bided its time before intervening directly in the management of its acquisition. It was not until May 1985, ten months after the take-over, that it appointed Stevenson as chief executive. But Stevenson's first two months in charge, as we have detailed in the previous chapter, were to prove sufficiently traumatic to more than make up for Thorn's period of relative inactivity: they saw the departure of its two top American bosses, the abandonment of dynamic ram production, and redundancy for a quarter of the work-force.

In parallel with the internal turmoil, the early summer of 1985 also saw the revival of external uncertainty over the ownership of Inmos. As early as May 1985, the City was swept with rumours of a predatory take-over bid being plotted for Thorn EMI. The logic behind the rumours was evident. With its share price having crashed from its high of £7 before the BAe fiasco to around £4, the value of the company's assets looked like exceeding their market capitalisation. Furthermore, the wide range of Thorn's activities meant that it could be parcelled up into attractive packages which could be sold off separately by a successful bidder for far more than the cost of acquiring the whole business. The American music operation, for example, would be a tempting purchase for one of the existing American entertainment giants; and it is hardly surprising that RCA was persistently named as a potential bidder by the speculators.

Take-over rumours were intensified in September when three board members from the Laister camp resigned and it was revealed that Australian entrepreneur Robert Holmes à Court had bought a substantial shareholding through nominees. It was clear that, in terms of stability of ownership, the Thorn purchase had simply catapulted Inmos from the public frying pan into the private enterprise fire. Yet Inmos managers remained phlegmatic about the bid rumours. Peter Cavill, for example, by 1985 director of microcomputer products, remarked: 'any new owner would have no option but to follow Thorn's policy of hanging on and waiting for the company to start earning money again'.

So despite seven years of struggle and drama, the political and economic factors determining Inmos's future had not altered much since the Callaghan Labour Government accepted the challenge of trying to take on the Americans in the efficient manufacture of standard, high-technology chips in 1978. Every Labour manifesto since 1964 had contained pledges to carry through massive programmes for modernising and strengthening British industry. Yet most of these promises failed to be turned into workable policies and each failure had been accompanied by a fresh attempt to produce a satisfactory analysis of the problems associated with exercising public control over private industry in a mixed economy.

By the late 1970s, political attention was firmly focused on the apparent inability of British financial institutions to provide adequate resources for high-technology enterprises. Other industrialised countries were apparently able to find money for the foundation and nurturing of the kind of sunrise companies which, it was argued, held the key to participation in the future of industrial manufacturing. But in Britain, it seemed, investment was just not available for schemes that entailed high commercial risk. It did not take any very fancy footwork on the part of the custodians of the City institutions to sidestep this frontal attack, and they had remained highly sceptical of the commercial or strategic need, for example, for British industry to make high-volume chips. But the main defence put up by the City establishments to Labour criticism was that they had examined such proposals as those put up by the Inmos founders and were convinced that they were not commercially viable. Inmos, the City had claimed, would inevitably have cost the

Government huge sums that it had no realistic chance of recovering. The British financiers would not have backed Inmos because to do so would have been foolish.

Apart from the hostility of British financial institutions, the Inmos project had very little to make it unmistakably the idea of a Labour Government beyond the crucially important point that if it could be made to work it would be damaging evidence of the City's inadequacies. The Government put up the money for Inmos because the normal sources of finance in Britain either could not, or would not do so on terms that were workable. Nevertheless, the deal was structured so that the founders stood to make considerable gains if the enterprise succeeded, since the NEB was deliberately trying to copy the formula that had worked with conspicuous success when applied to such companies in the United States, with all of the implications this had about the organisation of the business.

The attempt to spread ownership of the company widely amongst the employees would have been normal with an American start-up. But a major difference between Inmos and its American counterparts was that in the United States the investment community did not automatically react to talk of a company becoming involved with silicon chip development by refusing to invest their money. The essential stability of the City's attitude to high technology was well illustrated by the reaction of the financial institutions to the news that Thorn had decided to buy Inmos. Although by 1984 the British chip-maker was demonstrably as credible as most established semiconductor companies, and was certainly regarded as a serious competitor by many of its fellows, Thorn's share price crashed.

As an isolated event this negative reaction could be explained. The immediate prospects for Inmos were not as bright as they were being painted and an astute investment analyst who anticipated the 1985 chip slump would undoubtedly have been doing a very good job, especially if a 'sell'

recommendation had accompanied the information. The City
reaction was, however, based not so much on premonitions of a
temporary, short-term decline and expectations of lower
immediate earnings, but rather on the perception that Thorn
was fundamentally in trouble. As a concomitant, rumours
started to circulate suggesting that the large Thorn institutional
investors wanted Laister's head.

Parallels were drawn with the fate of the senior management
at Rank, where revolt by its institutional investors had resulted
in a new management being put in. And these rumours, as we
have seen, proved totally accurate. Laister was accused of more
than mishandling the rights issue that followed the Inmos
purchase. It was made abundantly clear to him by his firm's
shareholders that buying a chip-maker was not the way to attain
a quiet life as a successful corporate chief executive. It had
never been easy for a company engaged in leading-edge
technology to find sufficient investment funds in Britain, and
Laister's experience demonstrated that even a large and well-
respected conglomerate can still find it hard to raise cash for
such purposes.

To be fair to the City, its analysts' early diagnoses of Thorn's
long-term malaise also turned out to be fully justified. The new
shares sold for £136 million in the July 1984 rights issue had
been offered on the basis of informed, pre-tax profits
projections of around £186 million for the 1984/85 financial
year. In the event, only £108 million was achieved which did
not include a £21 million exceptional loss incurred by Inmos's
abandonment of dram production. For 1985/86, earnings
forecasts were progressively reduced from £130–£140 million
in the spring to £80–£100 million by autumn. Only a small part
of this expected profit decline would be blamed on Inmos's
problems during the chip slump.

The relationship between a quoted company and stock-
brokers' analysts is so close that it can be described as
incestuous. The main task of the analysts is to predict profits

accurately and they do their job, usually, with the full connivance of the firms whose performance they monitor. When the analysts, and other commentators, feel they have been misled, as they did with a vengeance in the case of Thorn's rights issue, their displeasure knows no bounds, and the results of their retaliatory actions can be catastrophic for the managements they believe to be guilty of what for them is the ultimate sin — failing to signal a change in a company's fortunes.

The City of London, nevertheless, does not emerge with much credit from the Inmos saga, and the Conservative Party does not come out of the privatisation story with very much more, at least not according to its own criteria. Inmos's performance had been as entrepreneurial as any right-wing Conservative could have wished it to be. At the time of its sale to Thorn, the firm was making money and wanted to remain independent. Two schemes to enable it to remain outside the clutches of a large company were well advanced and all of its staff were in favour of one or the other. Yet for the sake of reducing the Public Sector Borrowing Requirement by £125 million the Inmos experiment was abandoned and sold to an established business.

If it is desirable to make the economic and commercial climate of Britain more like that of the United States, and in many respects Conservative Government policy is aimed at doing just that, perhaps it would have been prudent for the Government to have listened to the reasoned advice of a highly successful, commercially-minded American engineer. Shortly after the Thorn purchase, Heightley believed emphatically that it was vital for the entrepreneurial environment to be maintained if a semiconductor company was to prosper. He said:

People have got to be able to make a lot of money. There is no value in the share options available to our employees now. The real problem is that no established company has enough money to create the appreciation of share prices that the public stock market has. You have to be independent and publicly quoted for the shares to be worth owning.

Many of those in the company still believe this analysis to be correct: that a large injection of outside shareholders' funds would have been preferable to being acquired by such a large electronics group as Thorn, or any predatory giant which might, in turn, take it over. The ousting of Petritz and Heightley in July 1985, however justified on Thorn's terms, lends weight to the thesis that either a private British placing or a flotation on the American stock market, although both would have brought in less money, would at least have maintained the essential freedom of the business to operate in a manner which, however strange to the outsider, the rest of the semiconductor community would have regarded as normal.

If Heightley's views are correct, Inmos's future looks rather gloomy: the bright technological star stands a good chance of slipping into the dull, staid, lack-lustre stability that participants in British manufacturing know so well. Especially after Petritz and Heightley's sacking, the talented designers whose abilities are so much in demand and the business managers with specialist skills and contacts that are irreplaceable will look wistfully at the rival American start-ups that did go public and see their counterparts getting rich, whilst the best they themselves can hope for is a comfortable salary long into the future.

It is certainly possible to run an insurance company on the principle of minimising risk, but a major component of the Inmos concept had been that high-technology firms required the establishment of structures that allowed creative people to feel they had a permanent stake in the success or failure of their enterprise. After a typical American start-up went to the American stock market in 1984, up to a dozen of its top managers were worth around $2 million each. And many other employees did rather nicely in the eyes of their bank managers, at least until the chip slump hit in 1985. All concerned, however, would have felt confident that their fortunes would soon revive during the next semiconductor boom.

In contrast, although the initial return for holders of Inmos employee share holdings was probably higher under the Thorn agreement than it would have been if a minority flotation had gone ahead, many of them, especially the 'high flyers', perceived that their opportunity for personal gain was, regrettably, unique, and that for those who ought to be making the daring and difficult decisions in future on the company's direction the lure of capital appreciation had vanished. It is possible to argue that over time the best of the staff would have drifted away anyway as better chances came up and that their replacements would have fitted in more neatly to the quieter big-company environment that smart semiconductor outfits would regard as anathema. On the other hand, it is even more likely that the original Inmos concept would have been betrayed if the firm had become just another pushy American-funded independent.

Arguments about the best way of motivating the senior couple of dozen managers in a chip-making firm may only be of major interest to the individuals involved. But the ability of the company to provide secure employment for large numbers of less highly-prized people is, however, of far more general concern. The British Government thought it was going to create 4,000 jobs as a direct result of its investment in Inmos. In fact the company has never employed more than 1,000 in the UK and it seems unlikely that the original target will ever be reached. First, this is because labour productivity in the industry had increased dramatically since 1978. Secondly, Inmos has signed deals licensing both a Japanese and a Korean semiconductor start-up to make its 256k cmos dram and has subsequently abandoned its own efforts to manufacture this part. The

I know it's a long way to commute but you'll love the view of Mt Fuji.

Japanese NMB and the Korean Hyundai will therefore be the sole producers of this circuit, which is likely to be the highest volume Inmos chip ever, and thus the generator of the most jobs. Both deals earned Inmos substantial advance payments and the promise of a royalty on each part sold. NMB has invested £170 million in capital equipment and plant for the project and starting production will cost it even more. Large numbers of jobs will be created in Japan and not in a depressed area of Britain as the firm's original backers intended.

High-technology companies may not produce many factory jobs and, as the Inmos example demonstrated, even those that are created are not necessarily in the firms' countries of origin. The reason is beyond the control of the Inmos and Thorn boards of directors. While Inmos must pay around 20 per cent annual interest on money it borrows for capital expansion, NMB can finance its project at a rate nearer 3 per cent, through the long-term loans available to Minebea, its Japanese parent company.

Although Inmos sacrificed the employment generation potential of dram production, the decision to license its dram technology is, in business terms, very shrewd. As part of the deals it acquired the right to buy chips made to its designs from NMB and Hyundai at a guaranteed discount for resale under its own name. Bearing in mind the extreme volatility and competitiveness of the dram market, Inmos has thus avoided the need to fund a costly and speculative development programme, which would have to have been financed at crippling rates of interest, and still be able to achieve a secure stake in the dram market with relatively little risk.

In the light of the employment implications, the timing of the announcement of Inmos's agreement with the Japanese seemed to have been carefully chosen. It was on 21 June, three hours before Inmos was due to be debated in the House of Commons, and nine days after its sale to Thorn. Members of the Opposition, who had called the debate, congratulated

Inmos on the agreement and pointed out that it demonstrated how saleable its technology was. No one picked up the far more important point that jobs and investment were going to a facility in the Far East because Inmos could not get the money to put up factories of its own. But one could not blame Peter Laister. If he were to have committed Thorn resources to dram production, the institutions probably would have ousted him far sooner. Inmos would never have come to the United Kingdom in the first place had it not been for the temporary famine of venture capital in the United States at the time Petritz wanted to set up a semiconductor company. It is thus ironic that, seven years on, a similar capital famine in Britain forced the company to export its hard-won technical expertise to the Far East.

Apart from the hazards created by the 'boom-and-bust' semiconductor cycle, the biggest problem that will continue to face Inmos is the price of money in Britain which, of course, plagues other manufacturing businesses just as badly. In the case of Inmos there is no doubt that the operation would be larger today, would employ more people and would be more able to compete internationally if it did not have to pay more for its finance that either its Far Eastern or American competitors.

While both the City and successive British governments can be blamed for many of Inmos's operational difficulties, the latter, at least, did not do too badly out of the company. The taxpayers got their money back and, allowing for inflation, almost made a profit. In exchange for an investment of £65 million, about £8 million in development grants and £35 million of lease guarantees, the Government received £95 million and its guarantees were taken off its hands without ever being exercised. While the Government got a reasonable deal out of Inmos, the nation, and the industrial community in particular, did not fare so well. According to the Mackintosh thesis, developed back in the mid 1970s and used as partial justification for the formation of Inmos by the NEB, the establishment of a domestic mass-market chip-supplier was supposed to provide the rest of British manufacturing with a competitive boost. The performance of electronic equipment makers in particular, and the economy as a whole, would be improved as they acquired access to the latest chip designs before overseas users had a chance. But, at least before the advent of the transputer, this just did not happen. Over 80 per cent of Inmos's output went to the United States. Europe accounted for only 14 per cent and despite a mammoth marketing effort, British firms only bought about 3.5 per cent of Inmos's production.

On 1 October 1985, however, the Mackintosh thesis could finally be put to the test properly. For it was then, at the Institute of Contemporary Arts in London, that the transputer, the seven-year chip, was formally introduced. Following their London debut, the transputer launch team, consisting of Barron, Cavill and A.C. D'Augustine, the American marketing vice-president (the senior remaining American executive after the purge), embarked on an exhausting round-the-world trip to sell the benefits of the British chip to audiences in New York, San Francisco and Tokyo. The Newport plant had been busy for months producing the T414 chips in sufficient quantity to support the launch (the T414 is a 32-bit version with 2k bytes of on-chip sram). Ian Pearson, the man in charge of transputer marketing, was determined to convince the world that the transputer was a real product instead of just a figment of Barron's imagination. 'Before October the transputer still had a credibility gap,' said Pearson, 'but this started to vanish after the launch.'

Realising that the company had to make it as easy as possible for equipment designers already committed to more conventional processors to adjust to the novel and innovative features of the Inmos device, the T414 itself was not the star of the launch programme. Instead, the firm put together four versions of a printed circuit board containing one or more transputers and all the associated components needed to make a working system. These evaluation boards were to enable engineers to experiment with the transputer with the minimum of effort. They were produced in hundreds and sent to Inmos's distributors at the end of September.

One of the boards, for example, codenamed the B004, was designed to plug in to the world's most popular personal computer with electronics engineers — the IBM PC-AT. Software packages were produced to run on the IBM, the equally ubiquitous DEC VAX superminicomputer, and Inmos's own adopted development vehicle, the Stride workstation, to enable the T414 to be programmed in three well-established languages: C, Fortran and Pascal, as well as occam.

The decision to facilitate the programming of the transputer in widely-used languages represented something of a climb-down from the firm's initial purist intention to promote only occam. The three languages were, however, embedded within an occam framework to provide a fair approximation to what software experts regard as the holy grail — an 'integrated programming support environment'. By providing the facilities of an 'ipse', the Inmos team thus hoped to lure engineers gradually to appreciate the beauty of occam.

Despite the credibility boost given the transputer by its public launch and the availability of evaluation boards, one serious sales impediment remained: the lack of a 'second source'. It is customary for chip-makers to provide mutually beneficial alternative sources for each other's products in order to convince potential customers that their source of supply is not dependent on the fortunes of a single firm. Inmos, however, deliberately decided only to negotiate such a deal only after the transputer had already gained some market credibility in order to obtain the most favourable terms. In the conditions prevailing during the 1985 chip slump, the company had little option but to adopt this course.

Even without a second source, there were plenty of firms interested in the potential of the transputer long before its public introduction. Inmos had selected, and had been carefully cultivating, a dozen likely high-volume users of the chip since the autumn of 1983 when the very first prototypes had been produced. Early fears that only the military would be interested in the transputer were belied by the fact that eight of them made at least some commercial equipment. Nevertheless, in Britain the Royal Signals and Radar Establishment was the most advanced in its familiarity with the part, although it might be decades before it ordered transputers in quantity.

In spite of the symbolic significance of the London launch of the transputer, it nevertheless seemed that the chip's first volume users would be in the United States. 'There are so many companies over there with a very low inertia in respect to product innovation that it seems inevitable our first big orders will come from the other side of the Atlantic,' explained Pearson. At least one British customer, however, might still pip the Americans to the post. The building next to Inmos's Bristol headquarters houses a firm called Meiko. Set up only a few months before the October launch, this company, the first spin-off from Inmos, was able to demonstrate in August 1985 at a prestigious West Coast exhibition what the transputer could do. In just six weeks the six-man Meiko team flung together a computing engine built from 128 prototype transputers which astounded American audiences with its ability to implement hundreds of millions of instructions per second of a sample program designed to manipulate image arrays.

Inmos had obviously learned a lot from its early wrangles with Mostek. The Meiko team, led by David Alden and Miles Chesney, wanted to cash in their Inmos shareholdings and branch out on their own. Inmos responded by offering a lucrative contract to produce demonstration machines that would give it something to show off at the transputer's debut. Just as Mostek had persuaded its potential defectors to Inmos to set up Micron Technology, Inmos managed to turn the likely loss of many of its key staff to its own advantage.

Despite the enthusiasm generated at the ICA, Inmos executives were realistic about the transputer's likely contribution to the firm's stretched finances. 'It will take between six months and two years for the transputer family to generate a sufficient volume of sales to make any money for the company,' estimated Pearson. In the meantime, the company must necessarily look to an upturn in the commodity chip market to generate enough sales and royalty income to meet its self-imposed target of getting back in the black by the beginning of 1986.

If it succeeds, there is also, of course, massive potential for the varied divisions of Thorn to exploit other Inmos devices in a wide range of its products: from food mixers and satellite television receivers through to guided missile controls and telephone exchanges. Even the humblest of Thorn's consumer products could be transformed by an injection of Inmos high technology. Barron likes to talk half seriously of an 'intelligent' toaster made from two wafers of silicon. The wafers would provide not only the sensors and controls but also the heating element. 'That would keep Newport busy!', quipped Barron.

If the company had not yet done much for the outlook of the UK electronics industry and the economy so far, it certainly has done lots for the outlook of its neighbours in Newport. Inmos is the proud owner of a very impressive building, designed by the internationally renowned Richard Rogers partnership. Neither is the building in Colorado Springs exactly a tin shack around a clean room. Inmos has spectacular American accommodation. The buildings make statements about the company, and for that reason they were important: but they did cost a great deal of money.

Setting up two wafer fabrication plants with no products ready to put in them was a risky commercial necessity, but creating two of the world's finest industrial buildings could be viewed as extravagance. It is certain that cheaper buildings would have sufficed. But Inmos was no ordinary company and if the main object of the exercise was to produce a viable manufacturer that made money and good components, a subsidiary aim was to inspire the rest of British Industry, and impress potential buyers of the firm's permanence and commitment.

After the Thorn take-over, there was little doubt which of the two magnificent edifices was the premier. Barron had lost control of the Newport factory in 1983, together with all manufacturing, marketing and other activities in Europe. These were then controlled from the United States with the single exception of the Bristol design centre. By the autumn of 1985, the whole business was firmly in British hands with the American side running itself but reporting, if perhaps temporarily, to Thorn-appointed managers in Britain. After seven years of turmoil Inmos, with little help from its backers, had transformed itself from a rank outsider to a favourite in the world semiconductor stakes.

But sometimes even favourites can fall at the last fence, or they can be 'nobbled', or their owners may decide to sell them or withdraw them from the race. The transputer, if it only achieves a fraction of its designers' goals, may well do more for the British economy than the entire £350-million Alvey research programme, also intended to revitalise the economy through an injection of electronic wizardry.

The Inmos saga should therefore give hope and encouragement to many others in Britain who believe that a thriving high-technology sector is vital to the country's future as an industrial nation.

Appendix

Although the electronics industry is now regarded as the epitome of an up-to-date, high-technology sector, its origins can be traced back to the discovery of electromagnetic induction by Faraday in 1831. Two great innovations, the electric telegraph and the telephone, both concerned with the transmission of information by means of electrical signals, grew out of this discovery. By the end of the nineteenth century most of the industrialised world was connected by the telegraph network and few large cities were without a local telephone system. The industries that supplied these networks were, however, closely related in commercial and technological terms to the electrical industry itself.

The advent of an electrical supply network for lighting, heating and power grew up in parallel with the wire-based, electrical communications system. All of these relied on the harnessing of the 'brute force' characteristics of electricity: the ability of electric currents to create heat and light and of moving magnets to generate electricity. In contrast, the essential feature of electronics is its reliance on the delicate 'fine-scale' behaviour of electrical phenomena and their exploitation for practical purposes. Thus it is the radio rather than its precursors — the telegraph and the telephone — that must be seen as the first truly electronic product.

Wireless telegraphy was developed around the turn of the twentieth century by an Italian. Guglielmo Marconi, who came to Britain in 1896 in order to seek funds from the British Post Office. At first, as its name implies, the technology was only capable of transmitting Morse Code in the form of short bursts of radio signals (or electromagnetic waves). In order to be capable of transmitting the human voice, or any other natural sound, wireless telegraphy needed a reliable method of both detecting electromagnetic waves of a particular frequency and of amplifying the signal carried by such (carrier) waves.

Reliability in the method of detection and a mechanism for amplification of signals were attributes distinctly lacking in the first wireless sets. The first really widespread type took advantage of a property of certain naturally occurring crystals. These allow an electric current to pass freely in one direction but not the other. By doing this the information that was held on the carrier wave (by periodic modulation of its amplitude) could be fed direct to earphones. The so-called 'cat's whisker' radio worked on this principle. The listener adjusted a piece of wire touching the crystal until the best signal was detected. Although a big success with radio amateurs, the system was unreliable, incapable of amplifying the signal and unpopular with manufacturers.

The whole arrangement was quickly discarded in favour of a device that made reliable detection and amplification a practical possibility. It arose in the first decade of the twentieth century from a technology that had been developed by Edison, the pioneer of electrification, some thirty years earlier: the incandescent lamp. Professor John Fleming was working as a consultant to the Marconi Company in 1904 when he rediscovered a piece of apparatus left over from his earlier job as an assistant to Edison. This was an electric light bulb in which he had inserted a plain metal plate in addition to the lamp filament. (Edison had been trying to discover why his bulbs discoloured after use, and had put in the plate in an attempt to detect particles given off by the lighting coil.) Fleming discovered that if an electrical circuit was set up between the filament and the plate, an electric current would flow in one direction only. The property was just what was needed for the first stage in the detection of radio waves. Although Fleming patented the device for Marconi under the name of 'diode valve', the idea was not taken further by the company.

In the United States, however, Lee De Forest, working for the Western Electric Company, heard of Fleming's diode valves and persuaded a New York light bulb manufacturer to make some for him in 1905. Using the diode as a basis, De Forest added an extra plate, called the grid, which could influence the flow of current between the hot coil and the first plate. A small electrical signal fed to the grid produced a corresponding, but much larger, signal at the plate. Using a triode valve, as De Forest's device was named, small radio signals could be amplified sufficiently to drive the moving coil of a loudspeaker and the practical home radio was made possible.

Although the valve was a British invention, it was first to be commercially exploited in the United States. This was also true for the use of the radio for mass entertainment, and for many other subsequent elecronic inventions. The First World War gave an enormous boost to the development of radio technology. Both sides used it to send Morse Code and speech messages and the Germans transmitted entertainment programmes to the troops on the Western Front in 1917. So it is not surprising that with the outbreak of peace mass radio entertainment soon caught on. The United States was first to set up a regular public broadcasting service, with the KDKA station in Pittsburgh. It started transmitting in 1920.

In Britain at that time, the use of radio for entertainment was considered rather a frivolous application. It was not for another two years, in 1922, that the Government rather grudgingly consented to a pilot service to be put out by the Marconi Company. The idea caught on very quickly and by 1926 the Government had completely revised its opinion and had come to the conclusion that radio was far too important a means of communication to be left in the hands of commercial interests. It set up a system of public broadcasting in the United Kingdom, the structure of which closely resembled the BBC as it is today. By 1932, one and a half million wireless sets were sold in Britain, just ten years after the first transmission by a commercial station. An important factor in this rapid growth was the price of the sets themselves. The use of the valve as both detector and amplifier meant that early receivers could be bought for as little as 10/6d (approximately 58p). With average industrial weekly wages at around the £2 mark, even the licence fee of 10/- (50p) was no serious damper.

By 1932 valve radios had become far more complex and sophisticated, the technology had changed and developed fast. As this happened prices rose because, even with mass production, valves were quite expensive to produce, especially the more complicated ones. As the technology for valves had sprung from developments in the light bulb industry it was natural for manufacturers of bulbs to diversify into the new product. The manufacturing techniques were similar and from the start highly automated. Both employed glass envelopes, into which components were placed, air sucked out and a seal applied. Hence companies such as Philips in Holland and Ediswan in the United States got into the radio business via light bulbs.

Companies in the electrical equipment trades also moved into radio. The General Electric Company (GEC) and Ferranti, for example, put the skills they had acquired in building electrical distribution frames and the connecting of cables to work in the area of radio production. Radio was one of the few boom industries of the 1930s and its growth continued unabated right up to the start of the Second World War.

The only other important electronic development during the 1930s was the struggle by a small number of researchers to produce a workable way of transmitting pictures as well as sound. With the increasing sophistication of radio circuits, these pioneers realised that it was feasible to send more than just voice signals. John Logie Baird had invented his electromechanical system in the very early 1930s. An experimental station was set up in 1936 but it was not a great success in Britain and, as it happened, the electromechanical system was in any case doomed. In 1936 broadcasts in fact alternated between two competing systems: the Baird one (the quality of which was awful) and a completely electronic, American invention, which had been thought up by Vladimir Zworykin and was adopted by the Marconi Company in the United Kingdom. The quality was much better and it proved to be the only practicable system. Television was shelved in Britain right at the beginning of the Second World War and resources shifted to areas where a more immediate return was perceived. In America a commercial station did start, but soon after Pearl Harbour, when the country entered the conflict, it, too, was closed down for the duration of the war.

Television development may have been abandoned during the war but electronics in general received an enormous boost. In contrast to the Great War, the Second World War was one of technology. The pressures that resulted in the radios evolving into ever larger and more complicated devices suddenly were reversed. With the need to put then into a whole range of vehicles, from aeroplanes to tanks, the smaller, lighter and less power-thirsty the radios were, the better. In other words, for the first time the direction of change was towards miniaturisation; people were looking for ways to make valves smaller and circuits more compact.

There was, however, a limit to which valves could be miniaturised, for they need a lot of power to heat up the grid, and glass is heavy and fragile. The urgent wartime need for smaller and more robust electronic components had stimulated interest in the findings of research in theorectical physics that had been carried out in the 1930s. Physicists had been looking at the behaviour of solids in the light of the quantum theory in an attempt to answer such questions as: why are metals conductors of electricity and why is rubber an insulator? In the course of the research some materials were found to have rather peculiar sets of properties, somewhere between those of conductors and insulators. They are called semiconductors.

One group of materials that fitted into this category was found to be the crystals used in the old cat's whisker wireless sets. Now, with a systematic understanding of exactly what they were and the principles on which they functioned such crystals were dusted off and revived. 'State of the art' radios at the end of the Second World War had smaller valves and a more compact design, but they also had an encapsulated and far more reliable crystal as a replacement for the diode detector. It was a great leap forward because at least one part of the circuit did not need to be heated up and was not made from glass. The new detector was called the solid state crystal detector.

Apart from radio, two other innovations came out of the war. The first was radar. Here radio waves were used not for communication from one place to another but rather to bounce off distant objects, back to the transmitter and thus reveal the position of the distant object. Radar used higher frequencies than were required for radio, demanded the development of new components and in general gave researchers a far deeper understanding of how electronic circuits worked. In terms of direct applications, radar was a bit of a dead end. It has obvious military uses and commercial applications for the control of air traffic but no others. Long after the war, however, a vital application was found for radar. The same high frequencies used to detect objects can be used to transmit much more information than is the case with a normal radio frequency. The same technology enabled people to build microwave radios in the 1960s which made, for example, satellite technology possible. It opened a whole new field of high-frequency telecommunication uses.

The second important electronic device arising out of the war was the electronic calculator. The incentive for its creation had been the need to perform calculations more accurately and quickly. Aircraft in flight had to be controlled, bomb-aiming charts and artillery tables had to be compiled or recalculated and, of course, if the codes the enemy used for communication could be broken, an enormous advantage in terms of military intelligence could be won. The basis for all of this was theoretical work done in the inter-war years. A theory for an electrical calculator had been developed at Cambridge by Turing and resources were poured into projects to produce machines that worked. The Manhatten Project to build an atomic bomb in the United States gave the Americans an extra reason for wanting fast calculating power. And, indeed, from all of the development in the United States came the world's first all-electronic, high-speed calculators. The initial designs relied on valves, occupied whole buildings, were staggeringly expensive and could only really be afforded by the military.

After the war work on miniaturisation, radar and solid state devices continued. From the point of view of the electronics industry, the last of these, work on the behaviour of electronics in solid materials, proved to be the most important. In the field of semiconductors, materials such as Gallium, Germanium and Silicon turned out to be the most interesting. At the laboratories of the giant American Bell Telephone Company in 1947 it was discovered that not only did the behaviour of these materials lie somewhere in between conductors and insulators, but also that they could be flipped from one state to another.

Researchers at Bell Laboratories were able, by putting together a sandwich of three intrinsic semiconductors with slightly different impurities in them, to make a device (which they called a transistor) capable of amplifying a signal in exactly the same way as a valve. The great breakthrough was that, whereas with a valve the whole apparatus had to be heated up to obtain a flow of electrons, with three sheets of semiconductor material (and a small wire to each), the same amplification could be produced without any heat. The device was an analogue of De Forest's triode but far smaller and with a minute power requirement. With its wonderful power to amplify, the age of the transistor had arrived.

The impact of the transistor on the radio and television industries was widespread and continued over many years. It accelerated the trend towards miniaturisation that had started during the war, although, in terms of quality, the early transistor radios — they were mass-marketed in the late 1950s — compared very badly to valve sets. The transistor's impact on calculators was far more profound. Apart from their other disadvantages, valve-based machines could only calculate for a matter of seconds before one of the many thousands of valves burnt out and had to be replaced.

The transistor transformed into a viable proposition not just electronic calculators but also a far more important machine, the computer. The first commercial computer was built by Lyons (the teashop owner) in 1953. About a dozen were sold under the name of LEO, the initials of Lyon's Electronic Office.

One might well wonder what amplifiers are doing inside a computer. The basic principles can be traced back to work done in mathematical logic and philosophy at the turn of the century by Gustav Frege and Bertrand Russell. They had demonstrated that all arithmetic could be reduced to logic: any problem connected to number theory can be expressed in terms of logical statements that deal only in terms of truth and falsity. Applied to calculating machines, instead of having to cope with cogs and wheels to accommodate a ten-digit number system, all arithmetic can be performed with switches. 'On' equals true, 'off' equals false. Given enough space, the most complex of calculations can be done with a system of sluice gates of the type the ancient Egyptians used to irrigate the lower Nile basin; or any other mechanical, electrical or electronic system of switches will do.

The reason for using valves in a computer was that they were good switches. Not only could they amplify a signal, they could also switch it on and off very fast, at the speed electrons move. Compared to their use in radio, valves had a rather humble function inside a computer; they were not wanted as elegant amplifiers here, but just as very quick switches. The transistor brought all of its advantages over the valve to this job as well. It is important here to spell out the distinction between calculators and computers. A calculator is only able to perform a predefined set of functions. When required to do so it will add, subtract, divide or in some other way alter numbers. A computer is a calculator that is able to store a series of these instructions and then is capable of acting on them. The notion of having the facility to store the instructions in the same form as the information to be manipulated was itself as significant as the development of the transistor for the concept of the computer. At first the instructions were held as a series of holes punched in cards that could be converted into electronic form; later they were held directly in electronic form.

The first commercial computers came out in the early 1950s. They were only made in small quantities and were still expensive to produce. Although LEO was the first of its kind, only a few machines were sold, and the American business equipment company IBM was soon in the market with a more popular version of essentially the same product. The production cost of early computer manufacture stemmed from the assembly problem. Wiring together sufficient transistors to form a nucleus with enough complexity to be capable of reading instructions and taking in some information and manipulating that information in accordance with the instructions were both tasks of daunting complexity. Roughly 10,000 switches, or transistors, are needed in such a nucleus.

The computer had, by the early 1960s, become the driving technology of the whole electronics industry, in exactly the same way as the radio had been before the war. As with the radio, all of the industrialised countries had their own manufacturing capabilities, turning out much the same sorts of goods. In Britain, LEO was still in business; EMI, Marconi and many other companies also had a share of the growing market.

Through a series of mergers, Electric Leo Marconi was formed. This company finally merged with ICT (already a merger of Power–Samas Accounting Machine Co. and the British Accounting and Tabulating Machine Co.) to form ICL in 1968, under the Ministry of Technology which at the time was headed by Tony Benn.

Until the end of the 1950s the computer industry, although increasingly influential, was still not a very big business and despite some rapid growth the market was comparatively small. By the end of that decade, however, a development in transistor technology had changed everything. Inside the nucleus of roughly 10,000 transistors the basic computer sub-unit was four switches wired together. (Four switches of some sort are required for a single logical step on the pattern worked out by Frege, Russell and the other mathematical philosophers.) Throughout the 1950s these so-called 'logic gates' (the sub-unit of four switches) were made up of separate germanium-based transistors wired together.

The breakthrough with transistors came from work done by Hoerni at the Fairchild Camera and Instrument Company in the United States. He was experimenting with methods of making transistors from silicon, which involved a process that was not as straightforward as that used for germanium devices but had a number of advantages, including the production of parts with a wider range of operating temperatures. The motivation for Hoerni's interest in making transistors from silicon was that, with a wider temperature range, it should have been possible to sell lots more to the military. Hoerni found that with silicon it was possible to diffuse a layer of impurities on to a flat sheet (wafer) and then to diffuse a second layer of impurities on top of the firt one. The result is a sandwich of semiconductor materials of the kind needed to make a transistor. The wafer can then be cut up to make a larger number of individual transistors (or chips). But, and this is the crucial point, in this way they could be reliably mass-produced.

Robert Noyce of Fairchild and Jack Kilby of Texas Instruments went further. Rather than cut up the large wafer and then have to wire four of the little pieces together again to make a logic gate, Noyce and Kilby showed it was possible to put photographic masks over the wafer of silicon and use photosensitive chemicals and processing to produce layers of impurity only in certain areas, and hence to make a pattern. By doing this it was possible to build the four interconnected transistors together into a logic gate at the production phase and then cut up the whole sub unit as a single piece. This was the birth of the integrated circuit, commonly known as the silicon chip. On this single, quite simple development the whole of modern electronics depends. By refining the printing process by which the impurities and connecting layers are diffused on the wafers, increasingly complex and intricate patterns could be built up.

By 1962 up to one hundred transistors were being put together in one piece, to give a single chip, solid-state unit capable of performing arithmetic operations all on its own. Fourteen years after the first integrated circuit, a single logic gate, had been made, the magic figure of 10,000 transistors on a single piece of silicon was reached. The core of a computer could be built in a chip. These days the process of integrated circuit manufacture is well defined. The starting-point is a polished piece of pure silicon. A single crystal is placed on the end of a shaft and then rotated through a bath of molten silicon. A large, cylindrical crystal is formed which follows the exact structure of the one on the end of the shaft. The cylinder is sliced into wafers with diamond saws. The cut surfaces are etched chemically to give the appearance of a mirror. The thin, round wafers of silicon with their characteristic shiny surface are now ready to be turned into integrated circuits by the semiconductor makers.

The production, or fabrication, process is highly complex but has three basic stages: imagining, where the photographic patterns are transferred on to the surface of the wafer, is the first. Then the various layers of semiconductive materials are deposited and grown on the wafer. Finally come etching and masking operations in which the deposited layers are selectively removed or added to. The cycle has to be repeated many times to make a complete integrated circuit. Before photolithography the wafers are coated with a layer of photoresist. The process has to be carried out in a highly controlled, clean-room environment where dust is kept to an absolute minimum, all fumes are efficiently removed and the operators wear clothing that would look more appropriate on a space walker than a factory worker. The objective is to produce on the wafer surfaces a uniform, defect-free layer of photosensitive masking material.

The photosensitive material can at this stage be exposed to a very strong light. The positioning of the mask between the light source and the resist will, if it is done correctly, result in the pattern of the mask being transferred. Again it is very important that the environment for this stage is clean, as contamination on either the wafer or the mask will show up on the final developed image. When the exposed wafer is developed, the developer selectively removes either the exposed regions (positive resist) or the unexposed regions (negative resist), leaving behind an image that will act as a mask during the etching processes. A series of masks are applied and the resulting patterns etched away with new layers of semi-conductor being diffused on to the surface in between the two operations. Both wet (using acids) and dry (using a stream of charged particles called plasma) etching techniques are widely used, but the dry ones are more precise and are to be found in the more modern plants producing the most advanced semiconductors. The aim in etching is to remove the semiconductor layer left exposed by the developing process as precisely as is possible.

There are many techniques, sometimes called the 'black arts', associated with the etching process. These include special ways of placing the wafers in the etching medium, additives to alter the rate of reaction, and movement or rotation of the wafers during the process to ensure a uniform result. Properly etched wafers can proceed down the production-line and have new layers diffused on to their surfaces before starting all over again. In chip fabrication plants built in the last few years the conventional diffusion operations have given way to more ion-implantation processing, and chemical vapour deposition in horizontal tubes has been superseded by other techniques.

The object of both diffusion and ion-implantation is to introduce impurities throughout the silicon crystal lattice structure, thereby changing the electrical characteristics of the layer. A series of so-called doping, or diffusing, steps are used in the fabrication process to generate a set of profiles and junctions. These form the basis for the semiconductor devices. The process needs to be very precisely and accurately controlled. Ion-implantation is a technique that is used to place impurities at predetermined depths and with accurate control of the concentration. Its main advantage is the precision it allows. Chemical vapour deposition is a gas reaction process in which a large number of semiconductor layers can be formed by the heat-induced decomposition of gases. Instead of a horizontal tube, where gas is passed from one end of the chamber containing the wafers to the other, it is possible to use vertical systems. Here, with the gas flowing downwards and contained in a surrounding blanket of nitrogen gas, batch processes can be replaced with continuous ones. The wafers are carried along with a conveyor. Plasma deposition techniques have also superseded chemical vapour deposition recently. This involves the use of gases that are converted into very reactive chemical species with the aid of a radio frequency glow discharge. The gas plasma replaces the heat-induced decomposition reactions of chemical vapour deposition processes.

There have also been important developments in the area of

transferring the photographic image to the wafer. Early masks had to come into close contact with the actual wafer and this caused a whole range of problems. These difficulties were overcome by the development of projection printing, but problems with the depth of focus and spreading of the image replaced the problem of contamination from physical contact. Solutions to the most severe of these faults were found in the 1:1 refractive projector. Here, a carriage scans the wafer under a narrow beam of very intense light. The scanning continues until the whole surface of the wafer has been covered.

By the late 1970s scanning projection printers of this sort had established a dominant position in the semiconductor manufacture market. Then a completely new projection printing method emerged. Where the 1:1 printer used masks the same size as the desired final image, the step- and repeat-printer enabled the mask to be up to ten times larger than the final pattern exposed on the wafer. It is therefore possible to print down far finer patterns. So, one of the first applications of so-called 'wafer steppers' was the scaling-down of existing designs. The line widths it is possible to produce on the wafer are correspondingly narrower. Even finer lines, and hence even more dense designs, would be possible using electron-beam, direct writing systems. But these are said to be uneconomic at the moment and in any case there are still technical problems with the capabilities of the e-beam resists.

At present it is imaging techniques that have to be refined before more complex designs with even smaller line widths can be brought into use. As a result a great deal of attention is being paid by semiconductor technologists to wafer steppers and their associated equipment. Developments in imaging techniques, and semiconductor process equipment in general, affect the economics and technology of chip production in two ways. Firstly, the techniques change very quickly and in directions that make yet more powerful chips technically possible. Second, each new generation of equipment tends to be more

'I wish this stuff wouldn't go out of date so quickly.'

expensive than its predecessor and without the latest equipment a producer soon finds it impossible to compete.

Semiconductors may, as we have seen, be regarded as sophisticated switches but it is important to carry the story a little further. There are two basic families of semiconductor device, and movements from one technology to the other have important implications for the economics and profitability of a manufacturer. The older technology is that of bipolar circuits and it is still widely used. But in the past few years many integrated-circuit manufacturers have been attracted to the second family that employ so-called metal-oxide semiconductor fabrication methods. There are advantages and drawbacks to using either family.

Designers want to build ever faster, more complex and less power-hungry processors and memory chips. The basic decisions companies take on which kind of process to put into a plant will radically affect the options available to them. Speed, low power consumption and the ability to get more and more units on to a single piece of silicon are to some extent not compatible given the technical limits of the chip families. The frontiers are constantly being pushed further forward. Metal-oxide silicon (mos) devices already account for more than half of the dollar market for semiconductors, and by the end of the 1980s the proportion is expected to reach close to two-thirds. The member of the mos family of technologies that is growing fastest and is most responsible for the drift away from bipolar technology is complementary mos, or cmos. Here, and with other technologies, the main emphasis is on the size of the line width that it is possible to produce. The narrower the actual channels that are etched on to the silicon, the more it will be possible to cram on to a given area and ultimately the cheaper the function on the chip will be to be customer. Silicon designers measure these widths in units of a micron, or 1/1000 of 1mm. So, for example, a 2 micron process will be one employing line widths of 2/1000 of 1mm.

By the beginning of the next decade, chip-makers confidently expect to be making chips containing features whose dimensions can only be measured in tiny fractions of microns. By then, therefore, perhaps the industry will be forced to adopt a fresh set of equally esoteric units. Inmos may well be one of the pioneers of the sub-micron chip.